CONSEQUENCES

THE RISE OF A
FRACTURED WORLD ORDER

WILLIAM PRIEST | **DAVID ROCHE** | **ALEX MICHAILOFF**

WILEY

Copyright © 2025 by John Wiley & Sons, Inc. All rights reserved, including rights for text and data mining and training of artificial intelligence technologies or similar technologies.

Published by John Wiley & Sons, Inc., Hoboken, New Jersey.
Published simultaneously in Canada.

No part of this publication may be reproduced, stored in a retrieval system, or transmitted in any form or by any means, electronic, mechanical, photocopying, recording, scanning, or otherwise, except as permitted under Section 107 or 108 of the 1976 United States Copyright Act, without either the prior written permission of the Publisher, or authorization through payment of the appropriate per-copy fee to the Copyright Clearance Center, Inc., 222 Rosewood Drive, Danvers, MA 01923, (978) 750-8400, fax (978) 750-4470, or on the web at www.copyright.com. Requests to the Publisher for permission should be addressed to the Permissions Department, John Wiley & Sons, Inc., 111 River Street, Hoboken, NJ 07030, (201) 748-6011, fax (201) 748-6008, or online at http://www.wiley.com/go/permission.

The manufacturer's authorized representative according to the EU General Product Safety Regulation is Wiley-VCH GmbH, Boschstr. 12, 69469 Weinheim, Germany, e-mail: Product_Safety@wiley.com.

Trademarks: Wiley and the Wiley logo are trademarks or registered trademarks of John Wiley & Sons, Inc. and/or its affiliates in the United States and other countries and may not be used without written permission. All other trademarks are the property of their respective owners. John Wiley & Sons, Inc. is not associated with any product or vendor mentioned in this book.

Limit of Liability/Disclaimer of Warranty: While the publisher and the authors have used their best efforts in preparing this work, including a review of the content of the work, neither the publisher nor the authors make any representations or warranties with respect to the accuracy or completeness of the contents of this work and specifically disclaim all warranties, including without limitation any implied warranties of merchantability or fitness for a particular purpose. Certain AI systems have been used in the creation of this work. No warranty may be created or extended by sales representatives, written sales materials or promotional statements for this work. The fact that an organization, website, or product is referred to in this work as a citation and/or potential source of further information does not mean that the publisher and authors endorse the information or services the organization, website, or product may provide or recommendations it may make. This work is sold with the understanding that the publisher is not engaged in rendering professional services. The advice and strategies contained herein may not be suitable for your situation. You should consult with a specialist where appropriate. Further, readers should be aware that websites listed in this work may have changed or disappeared between when this work was written and when it is read. Neither the publisher nor authors shall be liable for any loss of profit or any other commercial damages, including but not limited to special, incidental, consequential, or other damages.

For general information on our other products and services or for technical support, please contact our Customer Care Department within the United States at (800) 762-2974, outside the United States at (317) 572-3993 or fax (317) 572-4002.

Wiley also publishes its books in a variety of electronic formats. Some content that appears in print may not be available in electronic formats. For more information about Wiley products, visit our web site at www.wiley.com.

Library of Congress Cataloging-in-Publication Data:

Hardback ISBN: 9781394339372
ePDF ISBN: 9781394339396
ePUB ISBN: 9781394339389

Cover Image(s): © Chuhail/Getty Images, © erhui1979/Getty Images
Cover Design: Wiley

SKY10122912_072525

TABLE OF CONTENTS

PREFACE	IX
ABOUT THE AUTHORS	XIII
ACKNOWLEDGMENTS	XV

CHAPTER ONE
    EXTERNAL CHALLENGES   1

CHAPTER TWO
    INTERNAL DEMOCRATIC DECAY   29

CHAPTER THREE
    POPULISM   43

CHAPTER FOUR
    SOCIAL MEDIA AND THE NETWORK EFFECT   61

CHAPTER FIVE
    THE AI OF IT ALL   81

CHAPTER SIX
    LIVING IN THE GRAYZONE   101

CHAPTER SEVEN
    THE NOT SO MIGHTY GREENBACK   121

TABLE OF CONTENTS

CHAPTER EIGHT
    IMMIGRATION   133

CHAPTER NINE
    THE HEART OF THE MATTER   143

CHAPTER TEN
    THE LAST CHAPTER   151

NOTES   165
INDEX   179

"There are decades where nothing happens; and there are weeks where decades happen."

– Vladimir Ilyich Lenin

PREFACE

The vision of a liberal democratic world order that emerged after the Cold War, which led to a brief era of major United States global dominance, is coming to an end. The fall of the Berlin Wall left a void, in which the US became the dominant global power. This "unipolar" world was supposed to be global in scale: oriented to capitalistic markets allocating the world's "scarce resources," commonly referred to as "land, labor, and capital" in Economics 101 courses. At this time, democratic regimes were on the rise, and the list of countries pursuing democratic policies began to grow rapidly.

Francis Fukuyama described this phenomenon in his 1992 book *The End of History and the Last Man*. However, this idea of a globalized world centered upon a mix of capitalistic principles and democratic ideals never truly materialized. While that seismic shift in history is behind us, its ripple effects continue to shape the challenges we face today. Democracy and civilization now stand at a crossroads, confronted by complex and daunting obstacles.

What was once a relatively stable geopolitical landscape has been replaced by a multi-polar world of competing economic and political powers. Today, democracy is under pressure from both internal and external forces, and this book focuses on these twin challenges. What caused these challenges, and what consequences will follow?

PREFACE

Externally, *Grayzone* warfare, defined as the use of hostile measures just short of war itself, pits alliances of autocratic and democratic nations against each other, reshaping global economic and political norms. The erosion of globalization and the rise of protectionism, two hallmarks of a fragmenting world, further strain international cooperation. At the same time, China's economic growth, once a key driver of global prosperity, faces significant challenges. Its heavy reliance on state-driven investment and structural inefficiencies may lead to a prolonged period of stagnation, disrupting global economic stability.

Internally, the rise of populism feeds on economic discontent, amplifying divisions within democratic societies. Populist policies often prioritize short-term political gains over sustainable economic reforms, undermining institutions in the process. Adding to these pressures is the expansion of the "Big State," as governments take on an outsized role in managing economies, risking inefficiencies from arbitrary capital allocation processes and unsustainable fiscal policies. These internal dynamics weaken the resilience of democracies and hinder their ability to adapt to global challenges.

Some may view this moment in history as part of an inevitable cycle, where democracy, like past systems such as the Roman Empire, feudal monarchies, or colonial empires, will face decline and be replaced by alternative forms of governance. This perspective suggests that the current challenges we face mark the beginning of the end for democracy.

However, this book asserts otherwise; the values and institutions of democracy can endure, but only if we confront democracy's vulnerabilities directly. To reverse democratic decline, it is essential to identify its root causes and develop cohesive strategies that address the structural issues undermining both its durability and stability.

A key to strengthening democracy lies in addressing wealth inequality by ensuring that economic gains are distributed more equitably. True wealth goes beyond simple measures like Gross Domestic Product (GDP) or national income—it represents a lasting "stock" of value rather than just a temporary "flow." Achieving equitable distribution requires creating systems that reward effort and innovation while avoiding over-reliance on entitlement, thus striking a balance that fosters both fairness and motivation. The tools to address democracy's challenges are already within reach, offering a reason for hope. However, significant hurdles remain, as we as a society often lack the willingness to act upon these solutions. While the potential for a stronger, more equitable future exists, achieving it will require overcoming the deep political and societal divisions that stand in the way.

ABOUT THE AUTHORS

William Priest

William Priest is a recognized professional in the asset management industry, with over five decades of experience creating and leading investment firms. He currently is Vice Chair of TD Wealth and Chair of TD Epoch, an asset management firm he founded in 2004 and sold to TD Bank in 2013.

Before founding Epoch, he was Chairman and CEO of Credit Suisse Asset Management, Americas from 1981–2001, and CEO and Portfolio Manager of its predecessor firm, BEA Associates, beginning in 1972. During his tenure at BEA and Credit Suisse Asset Management, he developed the firm into a respected investment manager with over $100 billion of assets under management.

He is the author of several published articles and papers on investing as well as three books—*The Financial Reality of Pension Funding Under ERISA*; *Free Cash Flow and Shareholder Yield: New Priorities for the Global Investor*; and *Winning at Active Management – The Essential Roles of Culture, Philosophy, and Technology*.

He is a graduate of Duke University (AB) and the University of Pennsylvania's Wharton Graduate School of Business (MBA) and holds

CFA and CPA designations. He is a member of the Barron's Roundtable and the Council on Foreign Relations.

David Roche

David Roche was born in Ireland, which he left as soon as possible with ambitions to write. He studied at Trinity University, INSEAD, and also obtained a CFA and C Dip Af. He founded Quantum Strategy, a subscription based economic advisory platform which creates products designed for the needs of clients such as those managing assets, needing to forecast markets, and/or evaluate geopolitical risks. Before setting up Quantum Strategy he was a strategist at JP Morgan, Morgan Stanley, and Independent Strategy.

In David's own words, "My inspirations are tectonic plate shifts, like the Fall of the Wall; the Russian invasion of Ukraine; and the death of liberal economics and globalization. So, my mind fires up when history is no guide but creative thinking is. Where there is discontinuity there is value in strategic thinking."

He is the author of several microbooks:

- *New Monetarism* (2008)
- *Sovereign Discredit* (2010)
- *Democrisis* (2012)
- *Death of Democracy* (2018)
- *Quantum Economics* (2022)
- *Living in the Grayzone* (2024)

Alex Michailoff

Alex Michailoff is a 2024 graduate of Cornell University's Undergraduate Charles H. Dyson School of Business. At the time of writing, he is working as a financial consultant in New York City.

ACKNOWLEDGMENTS

Thought leadership books are never created alone, and this book required a great deal of discussion, organization, and patience among the authors, who were almost never in the same geographic location or even the same time zone.

We would like to thank all the people who contributed to the creation of this book.

We are indebted to the publication team at Wiley: Bill Falloon for his guidance throughout the publication process, and Susan Cerra and Katherine Cording for their essential support along the way. We also extend our appreciation to Susanna Matson and Bala Shanmugasundaram from Wiley for their assistance and collaboration.

Special thanks to Jade Myers for his outstanding graphic design work, and to Matthew Michailoff for his invaluable help with organization, graphics, and overall coordination.

This book would not have been possible without your contributions. Thank you.

CHAPTER ONE

EXTERNAL CHALLENGES

Why write this book? With so many books out there, why this one? What makes it worth your time? Simply put, if you are reading this, chances are you live in a democracy, and that is exactly who this book is for—people in places where open dialogue matters most. In autocracies, books like this one often do not see the light of day. Information that questions power or explores uncomfortable truths is frequently suppressed, making free access to ideas even more essential for those who can still freely engage. In a democracy, the ability to ask questions, even ones without clear answers, is more valuable than in an autocracy, where answers are given but never open to questioning. Freedom of inquiry is essential for progress, while unquestionable answers only serve to suppress it. Questions that cannot be answered are better than answers that cannot be questioned. This underscores why protecting democracy is not just important—it is necessary.

CONSEQUENCES

Democracies represent freedom and the rule of law. Yet, if you live in a democracy, you are part of a system struggling to compete with non-democratic nations. This struggle plays out on two main fronts: from external forces and internal challenges.

Freedom and economic prosperity go hand in hand. A great example of this connection is shown in the Freedom House Index, which is available online for everyone to explore. Just look at Taiwan—a flourishing democracy and a key player in the global economy—compared to China, where freedoms are tightly controlled.

Taiwan, a vibrant democracy, achieved a high freedom score of 94 out of 100, ranking second in Asia and seventh globally in 2025. This reflects its robust political rights and civil liberties, contributing to its status as a key player in the global economy.[1]

In contrast, China received a low freedom score of 9 out of 100 in 2025, categorizing it as "Not Free." This score indicates significant restrictions on political rights and civil liberties, which can impede economic innovation and individual prosperity. It is no wonder that China is so interested in taking control over Taiwan, they would love to inherit its economic successes.[2]

While this example is extreme, we implore you to do your own research using Freedom House's free resources and see how your home country stacks up against others.

With so much economic success this begs the question: Why are our democracies losing their global influence to autocratic nations where citizens are not as free?

THE *GRAYZONE* WAR: DEMOCRACIES vs AUTOCRACIES

The rise of successful non-democratic economies in countries like China has given their government more political power. They pose a threat to democracies, especially in trade and governance.

Autocratic leaders often view democracies as weak and corrupt. They propose their own models for how societies and the world should be organized. What was once a world inspired by the spread of democracy, with the US at the center, is now one shifting toward competing visions of governance and alternative political systems.

What about the countries that have not yet aligned themselves with the democratic or autocratic ways of life? Most of these countries belong to what many refer to as the Global South, a group of nations primarily in Asia, Africa, Latin America, and the Pacific. They are often characterized by lower income levels and histories of colonialism or economic dependency. These nations encompass a wide range of political systems and development stages. Unlike the industrialized democracies of the Global North, many Global South countries struggle with structural inequalities and governance issues. However, they are also dynamic, home to rapidly growing economies, rich cultural diversity, and youthful populations.

According to the World Bank, within the next 50 years, one-third of the world's working-age population will be African.[3] Africa's expanding working-age population is seen as a potential catalyst for accelerated economic progress, provided that investments are made in education and employment opportunities. Where African nations, along with many in Southeast Asia and Latin America, align themselves in this new conflict, might end up determining its outcome.

Many Global South governments are tempted by the Chinese autocratic model. Why? Because most Global South countries are not democracies themselves. They dislike the nations which were previously colonial powers that make up most of the democratic alliance. They also envy China's authoritarian and meteoric rise to middle-income status. Since initiating market reforms in 1978, China has achieved remarkable economic growth, averaging 9.5% real Gross Domestic Product (GDP) growth annually through 2018, a pace the World Bank describes as "the fastest sustained expansion by a major economy in history."[4] This proof of concept has greatly aided China's case to become the beacon of hope for emerging economies in the Global South. China believes democracy will die of its own accord, but with a little extra push, it will fall over the cliff a bit faster (see our cover), and then there will be a new world leader and way of life led by a superior autocratic system, at least in their eyes.

The most important external threat to democracy today is the *Axis of Autocracies*. This includes primarily China, Russia, North Korea, and Iran. Opposing it is what we might call the *Alliance of Democracies*, which includes all NATO countries and Asian democracies such as Japan, Korea, and Taiwan. But the leadership is really just a single nation, the US of America. The US is by far the largest contributor to NATO defense spending, accounting for the majority of the alliance's total budget—reaching an estimated $755 billion in 2024, compared to $430 billion from all other NATO members combined. Beyond military expenditures, the US also plays a crucial role in NATO's broader

External Challenges

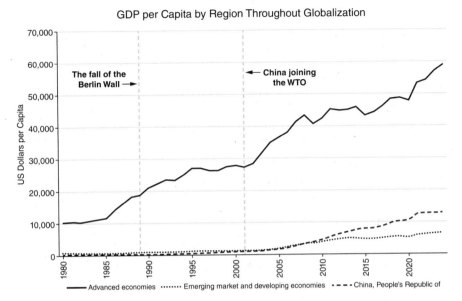

SOURCE: Data from IMF

initiatives, including intelligence sharing, logistical support, and financial contributions to joint projects and operational missions.[5]

The US's leadership within the *Alliance of Democracies* extends beyond its military and economic influence; it also lies in its historical role as a global promoter of democratic ideals. Post–World War II, the US established frameworks and organizations like NATO, the United Nations (UN), the International Monetary Fund (IMF), and the World Bank to solidify collective security, ensuring that democracies could thrive against threats such as the Soviet Union. Other US-backed organizations further reinforced this global order, including the World Trade Organization (WTO), the Organization of American States (OAS), the International Atomic Energy Agency (IAEA), and economic alliances like the G7, G20, and Asia-Pacific Economic Cooperation (APEC), all designed to promote trade, security, and diplomatic cooperation. The US consistently leverages its diplomatic and financial might to stabilize regions, foster alliances, and counteract the growing influence of autocratic states.

The *Alliance of Democracies* defends the existing rule-based international order. The *Axis of Autocracies* has its own alternative versions.

RUSSIA

Russia's ideology often ties its identity to historical control over territories like Ukraine, Belarus, and other Soviet-era states. This belief underpins much of its modern foreign policy and its attempts to reclaim the influence it lost after the Soviet Union's collapse. Under President Vladimir Putin's vision, the restoration of Russian greatness involves a return to the geopolitical dominance of its imperial and Soviet past. This includes undermining Ukraine's sovereignty, demilitarizing former Warsaw Pact nations, and even pushing for NATO's withdrawal from regions that were once within Moscow's sphere of influence.

Putin's speeches given in 2014, 2023, and 2024, along with his rambling propagandist theory of Slavic history published in his 5000-word essay at the time of the invasion of Ukraine, evidence his views. In his 2014 speech following the annexation of Crimea, President Vladimir Putin stated: "We are not simply close neighbors but, as I have said many times already, we are one people. Kiev is the mother of Russian cities. Ancient Rus is our common source, and we cannot live without each other."[6]

The consequences of this ambition are far-reaching. Russia's aggression in Ukraine—an area central to its claims of cultural and political history—not only leads to conflict but also destabilizes Europe's eastern borders. Kremlin-backed forces target Ukraine's critical infrastructure and civilian institutions to maintain leverage. Furthermore, Putin's rhetoric frequently references a grand historical narrative designed to justify actions perceived by much of the global community as violations of international law.

The devastating methods used to achieve Putin's vision are being witnessed daily in Ukraine. Russian forces have targeted civilian infrastructure, including hospitals, schools, and residential areas, leading to widespread destruction and displacement. Cities like Mariupol and Bakhmut have been reduced to rubble, and millions of Ukrainians have been forced to flee their homes, seeking refuge in neighboring countries or enduring harsh conditions in war-torn regions. These actions reflect not just a military strategy but an effort to undermine Ukraine's identity and sovereignty, fueling immense humanitarian suffering.

Instead of fostering stability, this expansionist strategy risks creating a humanitarian and political crisis across all of Europe. If left unchecked, Russia's actions could embolden further territorial ambitions, threatening the security of nearby democracies and undermining the post–Cold War order. While the ramifications are severe, they may not always involve overt violence; economic coercion and cyber operations are increasingly becoming tools of influence. This underscores the need for democratic alliances to counteract these moves with unified strategies. Alliances are both risk-mitigating and cost-sharing entities, something we will discuss later.

CHINA

China has a different approach than Russia. The Chinese plans for a new world order have been articulated in a trio of frameworks: the Global Development Initiative; the Global Security Initiative; and the Global Civilization Initiative. These initiatives collectively aim to redefine global governance and international relations in ways that emphasize China's vision for the future.

The Global Development Initiative prioritizes sustainable development and economic cooperation, proposing a model where development, especially in the emerging economies of the Global South, becomes the primary focus for international collaboration. While this framework claims to promote goals such as reducing poverty, improving education, and advancing green technology, critics point out that the lack of clear benchmarks and mechanisms for implementation leave room for ambiguity in its actual impact.

The Global Security Initiative, on the other hand, proposes a concept of security that is indivisible and holistic. It encourages nations to resolve disputes through dialogue and mutual respect while opposing military alliances and unilateral sanctions. This initiative positions itself as an alternative to Western security models, particularly NATO, promoting the idea that collective security should be achieved without forming exclusive blocs. Supporters see it as a constructive effort to reduce global tensions, while skeptics argue that it is designed to shield autocratic regimes from international criticism and intervention.

Finally, the Global Civilization Initiative emphasizes cultural exchanges and the coexistence of diverse governance systems. By framing itself as a champion of cultural respect, China promotes the notion that no single political or economic system is universally applicable, highlighting the flaws it perceives in the Western emphasis on liberal democracy. Critics contend that this initiative subtly undermines human rights and democratic values by framing them as culturally specific rather than universal.

Together, these initiatives reflect China's ambition to position itself as a global leader while offering an alternative to the US-led liberal world order. By focusing on economic development, cooperative security, and cultural plurality, China appeals particularly to nations in the Global South, many of which share historical grievances with Western colonialism. However, the inherent lack of accountability and the concentration of power within China's own system raise questions about how these plans would manifest in practice, especially if the values they promote come at the expense of individual freedoms and established international norms.

At the same time, China's expansive ambitions have not been confined to diplomatic initiatives. The country has pursued assertive territorial claims, including the militarization of artificial islands in the South China

Sea, repeated incursions along its border with India, and a strategy of creating economic dependency through its Belt and Road Initiative. These actions often blur the line between development and geopolitical influence, leaving neighboring nations and Western powers wary of China's intentions. While Beijing portrays these moves as steps to secure its territorial integrity and economic interests, critics argue that they represent a broader strategy of regional dominance that undermines international rules and norms.

NORTH KOREA

North Korea, the proverbial little sibling of the *Axis of Autocracies*, marches to its own drum—one that is nuclear-armed and eternally tuned to the praises of Kim Jong Un. Much like a younger sibling seeking approval, North Korea clings to its bigger autocratic "brothers," China and Russia, to ensure its survival. Its survival strategy is simple yet potent: keep the world guessing about its nuclear ambitions while leveraging its alliances to deter any existential threats. Pyongyang's security blanket is a patchwork of treaties, such as its arrangement with Russia, which promises mutual military support in the event of an attack. This dynamic might explain why rumors occasionally surface about North Korean troops showing up in unexpected places, from military exercises to foreign battlefields. In fact, North Korean troops have already been deployed to Ukraine to support Russia, marking a significant escalation in international involvement. This move aligns with North Korea's attempt to tie itself closer to Russia amid ongoing global tensions, offering workforce in exchange for economic aid or weapons technology. Such actions further complicate the conflict, introducing another dimension to the geopolitical stakes in the region. While North Korea's claims of nuclear fortitude often blur the line between fact and propaganda, they underscore North Korea's reliance on these alliances to punch above its weight in global geopolitics.

In the grand chess game of international relations, North Korea is less a queen or bishop and more like a mischievous pawn that occasionally takes the spotlight. Its role as a wild card is amplified by its strategic location and its ability to create headaches for the US and its allies. The regime's nuclear program not only serves as a shield against perceived threats but also as a bargaining chip in the high-stakes diplomacy game. Meanwhile, its cozy ties with China and Russia provide it with a semblance of economic and diplomatic backing, even as its economy struggles under international sanctions. For its part, North Korea offers its autocratic partners strategic leverage—acting as a thorn in the side of democratic alliances and a tool to destabilize regional order. Despite its small size and isolation, North Korea's antics ensure it remains a crucial, if irksome, piece in the broader puzzle of the global autocratic bloc.

IRAN

And then there is Iran—the self-proclaimed juggernaut of the Middle East, powered by a volatile cocktail of ideology, oil, and geopolitics. As a theocratic state, it wields religious authority to maintain internal cohesion while projecting influence across the region. Its ambitions extend well beyond its borders, using a combination of ideological appeal, proxy forces, and strategic partnerships to shape the regional order in its favor. For Tehran, religious fervor is as much a tool for domestic control as it is a banner under which to champion its anti-Israel and anti-Western agenda. At home, this fervor is paired with a state-controlled economy where systemic corruption enriches the elite, a fact critics argue undermines the potential of Iran's broader economy.

Iran's role as a regional powerhouse is amplified by its strategic alliances and resource wealth. With the world's second-largest natural gas reserves and fourth-largest crude oil reserves, Iran is an indispensable supplier of energy to its allies like China. Meanwhile, its partnership with Russia has evolved into a transactional alliance: Iran supplies drones and munitions that bolster Moscow's military efforts, while Russia reciprocates with advanced fighter jets, weapons systems, and other military technologies. These exchanges cement a relationship of mutual convenience, enabling both nations to counterbalance Western influence and sanctions.

Beyond its economic and military ties, Iran's influence manifests in its regional network of proxies. Groups like Hezbollah in Lebanon, the Houthis in Yemen, and militias in Iraq act as extensions of Iranian power, challenging rivals like Saudi Arabia and Israel. Tehran's deep involvement in Syria, where it supported President Bashar al-Assad during the civil war, shows its intention to remain a dominant player in Middle Eastern politics. Since the fall of Bashar al-Assad in 2024, Iran has withdrawn most of its forces from Syria, marking a substantial reduction in its regional influence. With the loss of an ally, Iran will surely continue to find ways to increase its power and stoke tensions, particularly with Israel and the US. Iran views its strategy as essential for survival in a region rife with competition and shifting allegiances.

In this intricate dance of power, Iran is both a disruptor and a stabilizer, depending on the perspective. To its allies, it is a steadfast partner, unyielding in its support. To its adversaries, it is a relentless challenge to the status quo. Regardless, Iran's role as a linchpin of the Middle East ensures that it remains at the heart of global conversations about energy, security, and the future of the region.

AN *AXIS* UNITED

The war in Ukraine has solidified the *Axis of Autocracies*. This group is now more integrated, coordinated, and dangerous than it was before Russia's invasion of Ukraine. It is no longer just a loose partnership where

China got cheap oil and minerals from a weakened Russia. Instead, it is now bound by a shared ideology and purpose: the defeat of democracy and the replacement of the current international order with its autocratic model. The members of the *Axis* also share a common belief about history—that democracies are doomed to fail because of their own weaknesses and excesses.

The alliance is further united by the way its new members have linked their military and industrial supply chains to support Russia's war. They have also made significant progress in improving how their armies, navies, and air forces work together during conflicts. In short, the *Axis* is now well prepared for coordinated military and political actions on a global scale.

Some may think that the *Axis of Autocracies* is nothing more than a patchwork alliance, held together by convenience and self-interest. It is easy to imagine that these countries—each with their own unique politics, economies, and goals—are simply using each other to achieve short-term gains, like securing territory or bolstering their defenses. Some will argue that such an alliance cannot last, since the differences between them are just too big.

It is like a group of neighbors who only come together to complain about a noisy dog on the street. Sure, they are united in their frustration, but once the dog moves away, they go back to arguing about whose tree is dropping leaves into whose yard. Similarly, skeptics believe that the *Axis* will unravel as soon as its members' shared goals—like opposing democracy or challenging the current world order—are met or no longer practical. After all, China's booming economy is vastly different from Russia's reliance on energy exports, and North Korea's obsession with nuclear weapons is worlds apart from Iran's focus on regional influence.

But here is the catch: even mismatched partnerships can stick around if its members see value in their collective strength. History is full of strange alliances that endured longer than expected, simply because the members found ways to overlook their differences when the stakes were high.

The question is not whether their politics or economics match perfectly—it is whether they believe they are stronger together than apart. And for now, their shared disdain for the democratic order seems to be enough to keep them working in unison. In the end, their unity is rooted in a simple truth: they stand stronger together, knowing that divided, they risk losing the power they seek to wield.

This alignment of power is eerily similar to how the Fascist Axis formed in the 1930s. Initially, it was a loose grouping that evolved into a unified alliance under fascist ideology. Despite personal disagreements, like Hitler's low opinion of Mussolini or his disapproval of Japan's aggression in Manchuria, this alliance nearly succeeded in overturning the world's democratic order. It took the combined efforts of the free world and Soviet Russia over 5 years and millions of lives lost to defeat the Fascist Axis powers.

Today's world faces rising risks of global war, with significant conflicts in Europe and the Middle East, and increasing tensions in East Asia. Much like the events preceding World War II, these regional struggles could intertwine, potentially overwhelming the international system and leading to a global security crisis.

Right now, these autocracies' (the *Axis of Autocracies*') perspectives on history highlight some challenges for democracies. Democracies are currently divided and sometimes hesitant in their responses, particularly in dealing with leaders like Putin. While the *Alliance of Democracies* is providing support to Ukraine, its efforts may seem focused on prolonging the conflict rather than decisively ending it. Clear and unified goals are lacking beyond Kyiv's immediate objectives.

If democratic nations fail to come together with a shared strategy and a stronger sense of purpose, they risk losing ground to the *Axis*. A lack of coordination or a retreat into isolation—especially if the US turns inward, away from its leadership role—could give the *Axis* the upper hand. But with greater cooperation and commitment, democracies have the opportunity to turn the tide and reaffirm their place in shaping the global order.

To highlight the stakes even further, consider what could happen if the *Axis* is not stopped in Ukraine. In the next decade, Russia might take further steps into Europe, seeking to expand its sphere of influence. This could involve establishing a "security zone" over several frontline states of the European Union, effectively dismantling democratic governance in these regions. If this scenario were to unfold, as many as eight democracies could lose their democratic status, representing roughly one-third of all democracies in developed and middle-income countries. This group includes Poland, Lithuania, Estonia, Latvia, Romania, Moldova, Serbia, and Georgia. Five of these nations are NATO members. To underscore the threat that these nations are feeling, consider this: all five are in the top ten member nations in terms of percentage of GDP defense expenditure for 2024, all well over the NATO guideline of two percent.[7]

This trend is not new—the number of democracies worldwide has been slowly declining for the past 18 years. However, a loss on this scale could deliver a devastating blow to the global democratic order. Organizations like Freedom House have reported consistent declines in democratic freedoms across the globe, with authoritarianism on the rise. Such a shift would not only weaken the principles of democracy but also embolden autocratic regimes to push their agendas even further.

There are also internal reasons why democracy is in trouble. Let us call them the "rotting pillars of democracy." These pillars, which we will explore in depth later in the book, have left democracies more vulnerable to internal decay and external pressures.

Democracies have developed deep structural flaws that, if not addressed, risk validating the predictions of authoritarian regimes. Autocracies argue that their centralized, top-down systems are more effective, particularly in times of crisis. If the democratic weaknesses persist, the systems of freedom and rule of law may find themselves eclipsed by authoritarian models that prioritize control and efficiency over individual rights and freedoms.

External Challenges

BACK TO THE COLD WAR

Let us go back to the period from 1945 to 1989. To understand where we are today and where we need to go, we must first look at where we have been and how we got here.

Between 1945 and 1989, the world experienced an unusually stable period known as the Cold War. This era began shortly after World War II, when the Western Allies realized that Russia was no longer pursuing peace and had become a rival rather than a partner.

What was the Cold War? It was a unique period in history—remarkable for the fact that it never actually became a war. The two superpowers, the US and Russia, glared at each other across the barbed wire of the Iron Curtain, always on the brink of conflict but never directly engaging in battle. Instead, they fought indirectly through proxy wars in regions like Asia, Latin America, and Africa. It was during this time that the term "proxy war" came into use—a term that, unfortunately, has regained relevance today.

There was stability between the US and its allies on one side of the Iron Curtain, and Russia on the other. It was what the Germans would call "Gleichgewicht," a perfect balance of power. They could spit and hiss like tomcats but not act. It was great! The stability of this period was underpinned by the concept of Mutually Assured Destruction (MAD), ensuring that while tensions were high, neither superpower acted aggressively. This was dissuasion by deterrence. It meant that if one side tried to nuke the other, the victim would wipe out the aggressor with its remaining missiles (often from untraceable submarines). It was a zero-sum game of lose–lose, instead of winner takes all. So nuclear war became a high-impact, low-probability event. In fact, the system was so stable that you could build your factory within two meters of the Iron Curtain and be quite safe.

Today, building a factory within 2000 kilometers of the Russian front in Ukraine would not guarantee safety. In fact, in 2024, US and German intelligence agencies uncovered and stopped a Russian plot to assassinate Armin Papperger, the CEO of Rheinmetall, a major German arms manufacturer supplying equipment to Ukraine. Meanwhile, Western officials have linked Russia to attempts to plant incendiary devices on cargo planes bound for North America, as well as poisoning Finland's water supply to disrupt and intimidate its population.

These actions mark a stark departure from the espionage of the Cold War, which often revolved around quiet exchanges of secrets in dimly lit alleys or cafés. Today, the stakes have escalated. Shadowy tactics have been replaced by bold and dangerous acts, reflecting a more aggressive and confrontational approach. That is the key difference between then and now.

In the Cold War, stability was made possible by the fact that there were only two nuclear superpowers. So, war never happened. That was until 1989, with the Fall of the Berlin Wall and the death of communism. Some, like Fukuyama, rather naively thought it was the "end of history," that a democratic alliance led by the US would prevail for centuries. Instead, it was the beginning of a new chapter.

For a while, it seemed like the world was entering a more peaceful and prosperous time. The US stood alone as the dominant global power, and many governments took advantage of this stability by reducing their spending on armies and military industries. People benefited as less of the economic pie was being devoted to "guns" and more to "butter."

This period had one electrifying effect: it added a massive wave of workers to the global labor force, as people who had been previously restricted under oppressive systems were now free to compete for jobs. This shift created what is called "labor arbitrage," where businesses took advantage of cheaper labor in newly opened markets, which became a driving force behind globalization. How did it do so well?

External Challenges

GLOBALIZATION

The answer is globalization—and its ancillary institutions like the World Trade Organization WTO - that set the rules for us to trade freely with one another.

Was it the right choice to allow newly freed workers to join the global labor market and give their countries access to international trade? It was probably inevitable, as excluding them could have led to wars, revolutions, and widespread instability.

However, one important factor was overlooked. Many thought that as emerging economies grew wealthier, they would naturally become more like democratic societies, governed by the rule of law. But this assumption turned out to be wrong. In reality, most of these nations became more authoritarian, not less. The Episodes of Regime Transformation (ERT) dataset identifies episodes of democratization and autocratization, utilizing data from the V-Dem Institute in Sweden. For 2023, ERT identified 42 nations that were shifting toward autocracy—close to an all-time high.[8] There were some exceptions, such as the former Eastern Soviet Bloc countries that joined the EU, but they were not the norm. Beginning in 1990 there was a sharp rise in the number of democracies. However, in the ensuing decades, their number has begun to stagnate and the number of autocracies, both elected and militarized, is back on the rise.

One factor, which could have limited the bad fallout of globalization, was ignored: we opened our markets to buy the products of "emerging economies," but they did not open their economies to our products nearly as much. Emerging economies, also known as developing or middle-income economies, are nations experiencing rapid industrialization and economic growth but still facing structural challenges such as weaker institutions, income inequality, and limited financial markets.

CONSEQUENCES

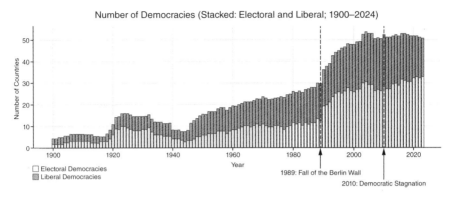

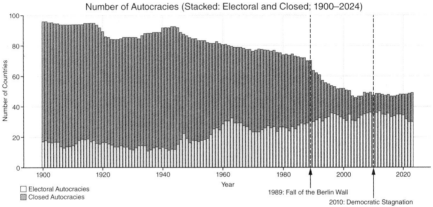

SOURCE: Data from Our World in Data

India, for example, has historically imposed high tariffs on agricultural and industrial products, making it harder for Western goods to compete. This imbalance created an uneven playing field where emerging economies enjoyed export-driven growth, while developed economies struggled with trade deficits, manufacturing job losses, and weakened domestic industries. This asymmetry proved detrimental to win–win scenarios.

Globalization allowed poorer nations to develop quickly by exporting to global markets and importing technology from more advanced Western countries. This trend lifted hundreds of millions of people out of poverty. China was perhaps the greatest beneficiary. In fact, its labor costs were so low that China became extremely competitive, quickly capturing a significant portion of the global market. China's share of global trade jumped from below 2.5% in 1997 to over 12% in 2022.[9]

Therein lies a principal flaw of globalization. Cheap labor from emerging economies priced the Western manufacturing workforces out of jobs.

Development theory suggests that economic growth follows a linear path, with countries progressing through stages from traditional to industrialized economies. In normal development theory, people usually move from one type of job to another as their country develops. It is a pattern we have seen again and again throughout history. Take China,

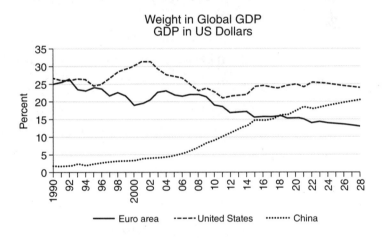

SOURCE: Data from IMF

for example: for decades, people have left farming to work in factories. Then, as wages rise and factory jobs become less common, workers often transition into better-paying jobs in the service sector, like healthcare, technology, or finance.

Let us illustrate how this new global interconnectivity works with an example. Imagine there are two countries: **Foodland** and **Clothesland**. Each country produces two things: **wheat** and **clothes**. However, their efficiency at making these products is different.

- **Foodland** is amazing at farming wheat. In one day, it can produce **10 tons of wheat**. But it is not very good at making clothes—it can only make **2 tons of clothes per day**.
- **Clothesland**, on the other hand, is fantastic at making clothes. In one day, it can produce **10 tons of clothes**. But it is not great at farming wheat—it can only grow **4 tons of wheat** per day.

Without Trade: If both countries try to produce both goods, they all spend a lot of time doing things at which they are not great. Foodland spends its time struggling to make clothes, while Clothesland tries (and fails) to produce a lot of wheat. Both end up with less of what they need.

With Trade: Now, what if Foodland focuses on what it does best—farming wheat—and Clothesland specializes in what it is great at—making clothes? They could trade with each other to get more of both goods.

Here is how it might work:

- **Foodland** decides to grow 10 tons of wheat and trade 4 tons to Clothesland.
- In exchange, **Clothesland** produces 10 tons of clothing and trades 4 tons of them to Foodland.

Now, instead of struggling to produce both items, each country focuses on its strength and trades. As a result:

- Foodland gets **6 tons of wheat + 4 tons of clothing** (more than it could make on its own).
- Clothesland gets **6 tons of clothes + 4 tons of wheat** (more than it could make on its own).

The Big Idea: The **Law of Comparative Advantage** states that countries (or people) should specialize in what they are relatively better at and trade for the rest. This way, everyone ends up with more goods and services than if they tried to do everything themselves.

The theory is that if every country does what it is best at, all countries end up richer. This is called the "Law of Comparative Advantage." It is a great theory, but only as long as labor forces are mobile domestically and internationally. Unfortunately, they are not.

In wealthy democracies, many workers lost their manufacturing jobs, because labor is much cheaper abroad. But instead of finding better-paying jobs in the service industry, like development theory would suggest, they often ended up in lower-paying roles or no jobs at all. At best, they went from earning decent wages on factory assembly lines to working for minimum wage.

Globalization for the rich democracies created both inequality and job losses without any new sector, such as tech, providing new, higher-paying jobs for the sort of people that were getting laid off.

Resentment over globalization grew out of the glaring inequality it created between those who lost their jobs or faced a steep decline in their standard of living, and those who could capitalize on the opportunities it provided. Consider this example: Mike and James, two neighbors, lived in a small manufacturing town. Mike spent 20 years working at a local factory, earning enough to support his family comfortably. But when the factory shut down and production moved overseas, Mike found himself out of work and unable to find a job that matched his skills or pay. Eventually, he took a low-paying retail position at a big-box store, barely scraping by. Meanwhile, his neighbor James, a savvy investor, put his savings into tech stocks and a booming Chinese manufacturing company. The returns allowed James to upgrade his car, renovate his home, and send his kids to college, while Mike struggled to keep the lights on. This stark contrast, repeated in countless towns and cities, fueled a deep sense of resentment. To people like Mike, globalization did not just move jobs overseas; it left them behind, creating a world where hard work no longer guaranteed success, while others thrived on the winds of change.

One author of this book grew up in a small Ohio town, Steubenville. In 1965, the population of Steubenville and the nearby community of Wintersville was just over 40,000. The town center had 95 businesses operating in a thriving downtown. There were three movie theaters, seven banks, and three department stores along with a nine-story hotel, the Fort Steuben, and the headquarters for the local radio and TV station. The economic drivers of this Ohio Valley community were its steel mills and there were three of them, the largest of which was Wheeling-Pittsburgh Steel, the ninth-largest steel company in the nation. It ranked #201 in the Fortune 500 magazine in 1968. In the 1960s, being a steelworker was a great career, and this allowed the majority of families in Steubenville to live comfortable lives. "The average steelworker's wage per hour in the early 1960s was approximately $3.00 per hour. That put the average steelworker (at that time) in the top thirty-four percent of US households. Their compensation allowed them to support a family, buy a house, drive a late model car, take vacations in Florida and send their kids to college."[10]

Between 1980 and 2000, the area lost more population than any other urban area in the US, and today its population is less than half that number. Much of this shrinkage reflected the declining fortunes of

Wheeling-Pittsburgh Steel. From its Fortune 500 magazine ranking of 201 in 1968, it fell to 296 in 1985 and then disappeared from the list altogether. Employment peaked in 1974 at 19,000 and by 1990 it was 6500.[11] Once the eighth-largest steel-producing company in the nation, went through several bankruptcies and reorganization. The last part of the old Wheeling-Pittsburgh facilities closed in 2022.

The cause of this? As globalization advanced, major industries began relocating abroad, particularly to countries like China, in search of cheaper labor and production costs. This shift led to the closure of local mills and factories, devastating communities that had relied on these industries for generations.

Today the downtown of Steubenville is a shell of its former self, with abandoned buildings and little commerce. Offsetting some of this decline has been commerce following residents as they migrated from the center of the city to the suburbs. What has really saved the area, however, has been the development of the College of Steubenville, now known as the Franciscan University of Steubenville. It is the largest employer in the city today.

The story of Steubenville mirrors that of many Midwestern towns, where the exodus of manufacturing jobs due to globalization led to economic decline and social challenges. The loss of these industries not only impacted employment but also eroded the social fabric of these communities, leading to a sense of loss and uncertainty about the future. The decline was further compounded by people fleeing to the suburbs, while retailers abandoned downtown areas in favor of malls, leaving once-thriving city centers empty and struggling to recover. In Bill's own words, "The community was devastated by the hollowing out of major industries, leaving limited opportunities for those who remain."

The expected outcomes of development theory—capital and labor moving freely across borders to create shared prosperity—did not play out as planned.

But one thing must be recognized about globalization: it boosted efficiency. It may not have been kind, but it was efficient. It produced goods more cheaply and with greater productivity than any other economic system. This drive for efficiency reshaped global supply chains, with countries specializing in what they could produce most cheaply and trading for other goods they desired.

No country embraced this shift more aggressively than China. By prioritizing industrial expansion and cost-cutting measures, it rapidly positioned itself as the world's manufacturing hub. China's efficiency gains, fueled by policies and resource allocation, turned it into the world's workshop, producing mass-market goods like textiles, steel, and electronics more cost-effectively than many advanced economies. These efficiency gains also extended to sectors like paper manufacturing, where in 2008 China became the world's largest producer, overtaking the US. China was able to turn from a net importer of paper products to a net exporter in a span of approximately five years, in part due to their low cost of labor.[12]

However, globalization is ruthless—efficiency drives decisions, and low costs dictate where factories are built. Dinny McMahon's book *China's Great Wall of Debt* describes this phenomenon well; "According to the Boston Consulting Group, by 2014, manufacturing in the US was, on average, only 5% more expensive than in China. In 2016, the American Chamber of Commerce in China found that a quarter of its members had either already moved some of their operations out of China or were planning to do so, primarily because of rising costs."[13] As wages in China began to rise and production costs increased, companies looked elsewhere for cheaper alternatives. Manufacturing jobs that once flowed into China started shifting to countries like Vietnam, Bangladesh, and Mexico, where labor was more affordable. This constant search for lower costs is a hallmark of globalization, ensuring that no country holds dominance forever.

This is important for two reasons. First, it has led to the stagnation of economic growth in China, which is a threat that we will discuss later in the next chapter. Second, it has led to deglobalization.

Deglobalization means replacing a highly efficient system with one that is less effective. Countries make this trade-off to ensure the security of their supply chains, so they are not disrupted by events like wars or pandemics. Sometimes, it is driven by the belief that having low-quality jobs is better than having no jobs at all.

Choosing deglobalization comes with costs: it creates a system that is more expensive, less efficient, and ultimately results in higher prices. However, this system is expected to offer greater stability and involve bigger government, which, in theory, will better support those who are struggling. Ultimately, that lowers standards of living. So, the pizza will be sliced up into more equal slices, but they will be smaller because the pizza will be shrinking.

The idea that globalization lowered living standards in wealthy countries is a myth. While it did harm certain groups, like workers who lost their jobs or saw wages decline, it did not lower living standards for these economies as a whole. In fact, globalization increased GDP per person in developed nations and significantly boosted prosperity in many developing countries that successfully integrated into global supply chains. For instance, a study by the Bertelsmann Stiftung Foundation found that from 1990 to 2018, advancing globalization increased Germany's average GDP per capita by €1112 annually.[14]

One reason for this is that even though China's economy grew much faster from a lower starting point, Western countries also gained. They benefited from cheaper goods, as China's exports consistently drove down prices year after year, improving real living standards for many in the West.

From the mid-1980s to the mid-2000s, Western economies experienced reduced volatility in growth, inflation, and interest rates, creating an era of relative economic stability. This period was known as the Great Moderation. During the Great Moderation, inflation in most Western countries fell from double digits to low single digits. Globalization played a big role in this by consistently lowering the cost of imported goods. This steady drop in prices helped many people, even those who had lost manufacturing jobs. While their incomes might have suffered, they could still afford necessities because everyday items became more affordable year after year. Recall our friend Mike. Even though he lost his factory job, he was still able to afford basic goods like clothes, electronics, and household items because they became much cheaper thanks to globalization.

Globalization also allowed China to develop great overall economic power and dominate a significant number of the most valuable supply chains, such as solar panels and electric vehicles. According to China's own industrial policy, it plan to boost self-sufficiency and has identified key industries for strategic development and subsidies, including energy-saving and new-energy vehicles, next-generation IT, high-end numerical control machinery and robotics, aerospace and aviation equipment, and biopharmaceuticals and high-performance medical devices.[15]

Let us take a closer look at China's role in the global production of another valuable supply chain: semiconductors. Semiconductors, or "microchips," are critical for a wide range of technologies from consumer electronics like smartphones and TVs to advanced aerospace systems such as satellites and Mars rovers. Taiwan, a US ally, leads the world in semiconductor manufacturing through Taiwan Semiconductor Manufacturing Company (TSMC). Meanwhile, China is investing billions of dollars and its top talent to develop its own semiconductor technology to reduce reliance on foreign chips. Both the US and China see controlling computing power as a strategic priority, especially given the importance of semiconductors in military technologies like guided missiles. Russia's technological shortfalls during its initial assault on Ukraine further highlight how critical these chips are. This urgency has led Chinese government analysts to argue that if tensions with the US escalate, "we must seize TSMC."[16] This underscores China's willingness to employ aggressive and unsavory tactics to dominate supply chains for critical technologies it does not yet control, further intensifying global competition.

The rise in the economic power of China also allowed it to project political power and increase its global reach. China's rapid economic growth, averaging 10% annually, enabled it to significantly increase military spending, far beyond what would have been possible without such expansion. In addition to improving the efficiency of the People's Liberation Army (PLA) through internal reforms, China increased its military spending. Because soldiers were inexpensive, only a small portion of the country's economic growth needed to be allocated to paying them. This allowed China to direct more resources toward creating new advanced military hardware. This shift caused democracies to lose their relative military dominance, as they struggled to match China's ability to achieve military advancements at such low cost.

Grayzone conflict between the alliances is not only about fighting for a bigger share of the global economic pie, but also competition for political and cultural dominance and the ability to project power. China has been able to do both simultaneously.

China has been upfront about its ambition to replace the democratic, rules-based international order with its own system. This model emphasizes economic growth and improving living standards, but it does not include democratic principles like voting rights. While it gives lip service to equality among nations, the reality is that this system positions China at the top, with countries in the Global South relegated to subordinate roles. In essence, it is a modern and refined version of imperialism.

These are some of the challenges democracies face. But external threats are not the only ones. There are also many internal trends which sap the ability of the democratic alliance to counterbalance or defeat the autocratic threat that it faces. What are some of those challenges?

CHAPTER TWO

INTERNAL DEMOCRATIC DECAY

Democracy is often thought of as self-sustaining, a system that, once established, will endure indefinitely. Yet history tells a different story. Democracies can erode from within, not necessarily through dramatic coups or revolutions, but through slow, incremental decay. The same institutions that protect democratic values can be weakened by internal pressures—populist movements, political polarization, and the erosion of civil discourse.

This chapter examines the forces that are undermining democracy from within, focusing on the rise of populism. Populist leaders claim to speak for the "real people" against elites, yet they often seek to dismantle the very institutions that ensure fair governance. As we will explore, when traditional parties attempt to counter populism through undemocratic means, they risk further corroding the democratic framework they aim to protect. In an era of rising discontent, understanding these dynamics is crucial to safeguarding democracy's future.

POPULISM

Populism emerged as a powerful political force, driven by ideas like anti-immigration and nationalism. Its rise challenged traditional centrist parties, which often made significant efforts to prevent populist movements from gaining power. But many of the methods that are used to keep populists out of power are not democratic.

In Germany, the Alternative for Germany (AfD) party—known for its anti-EU, anti-NATO, racist, anti-Semitic, pro-Putin, and anti-Ukraine stances—poses a significant political challenge. Traditional centrist parties are steadily losing voters to this far-right movement, which has gained alarming traction. Currently, the AfD is polling above 20% nationally and as high as 40% in parts of Eastern Germany. Even drawing comparisons to the Nazi Party, the AfD's rhetoric and growing influence have raised concerns about the resurgence of nationalist extremism in German politics. Its rise mirrors historical patterns, threatening the stability of Germany's democratic system.

How is the AfD firewalled? The strongest measure is through a strategy of forming coalitions between unlikely political allies. These coalitions often consist of diverse parties with little in common and no shared policy goals, united only by their desire to block the AfD from gaining influence, particularly at the local level. On a federal scale, traditional parties take an even stricter approach by refusing to include the AfD in coalitions or engage with them at all.

Blocking populist parties like the AfD from power through these coalitions comes with consequences. Many people feel their voices are being ignored, especially since these coalitions often lack any shared goals beyond opposing populists. As a result, these governments achieve little beyond maintaining the status quo, leading to frustration. This sense of being unheard pushes more people toward populist parties and the political extremes. This is a prime example of how democracy, by fighting populism and extreme ideologies, weakens traditional democratic parties.

Italy presents the opposite case, however. The Brothers of Italy party began as a far-right populist movement, known for its nationalist rhetoric and hardline stances, particularly on immigration. Initially viewed as a fringe group, it gained momentum by appealing to voters frustrated with traditional parties. However, after rising to power under Giorgio Meloni's leadership, the responsibilities of governing led to significant changes. Once in power, the party softened many of its extreme positions and adopted more traditional, centrist policies. This shift demonstrated how the process of governing can moderate even the most radical populist parties, transforming them into more conventional political players.

Of course, there are exceptions. For instance, the Brothers of Italy still maintain tough stances on immigration, showing little sympathy for migrants. This hardline approach has become common across much of the Western political spectrum, including among centrist parties.

A key takeaway is this: when populist parties gain power, the demands of governing often tone down their more extreme views. As a result, their most radical beliefs tend to become more superficial and less central to how they actually govern.

DISCOURSE

The second way in which democracy has sustained internal damage is in the weakening of the quality of its discourse. This is largely self-inflicted.

You might think that discourse is not particularly important, like differences in language—after all, we have tools like Google Translate to bridge those gaps. But that is not the case. If a family stops communicating, it stops functioning as a family, except maybe in terms of shared DNA. Similarly, if a society loses its ability to have meaningful discussions, it ceases to be a true society.

There was a time when debate was a cornerstone of society, allowing people with opposing views to engage in meaningful discussions. They could acknowledge each other's perspectives, maintain respect, and still stand by their own beliefs. A great example of this is the famous debates between Abraham Lincoln and Stephen Douglas during the 1858 Illinois Senate race in the US. These debates, held in front of large crowds, tackled critical issues like slavery and state sovereignty. After the debates, people gathered in their communities to discuss and reflect on the arguments they had heard. This tradition of open, respectful discourse not only informed citizens but also strengthened the democratic process by fostering a culture of thoughtful dialogue.

The misuse of social media has largely destroyed the tradition of meaningful discourse. Instead of engaging with diverse perspectives, people often only consume information from sources that align with their existing beliefs—a phenomenon known as confirmation bias. This leads individuals to seek out and accept information that supports their preconceived notions while dismissing or ignoring contradictory evidence. Worse still, repeated exposure to falsehoods on social media can make them seem true, creating echo chambers where misinformation thrives. This shift has eroded the ability of societies to engage in constructive discussions, further polarizing communities and making it harder to address complex issues.

Social media itself is not the problem—we are. Like a knife, it is just a tool. If you use a knife to cut your steak, that is perfectly fine. But in the hands of someone with bad intentions, it becomes dangerous. The same goes for social media; how we choose to use it determines its impact.

The misuse of social media has turned the old adage "seeing is believing" on its head. Now, it is more like "believing is seeing." People tend to interpret the world through the lens of their existing beliefs, often twisting facts to fit their narratives. This means that what someone believes shapes what they perceive as truth, making it harder to challenge misinformation or promote open-minded thinking.

We take in ideas which may be false, but if the "lie" is repeated often enough then it will become the "truth" in our mind. Then we will see the world through the prism of that false truth. Worse, we shall then only take in information that reinforces the opinion or idea we already have.

DEGLOBALIZATION

The third major issue is that the end of globalization is unlikely to reduce social inequality or improve living standards. Replacing optimized global economic systems with less efficient ones simply cannot achieve those goals.

Brexit in the United Kingdom provides a clear example of what happens when a country withdraws from a free market. The economic consequences have been severe, cutting off the UK from free access to markets that made up 40% of its trade. Beyond trade, Brexit has also created everyday inconveniences: UK visitors are now limited to 30-day stays in their European holiday homes, face long passport control lines, and must deal with complicated veterinary requirements for bringing pets abroad. A nation adopting deglobalization is like a partygoer who decides to stay home more often. At first, it might seem to be a safer and quieter option, but the partygoer misses the energy, connections, and shared experiences that come from socializing. Over time, this isolation leads to a loss of opportunities and mutual understanding.

For nations, turning inward not only disrupts trade and alliances but also stifles the exchange of ideas and resources that drive progress. Again, like decaying discourse, this is dangerous because it erodes the ability of countries to communicate.

Just like socializing at a party helps build relationships, alliances between countries are one of the most effective ways to share power and resources. Deglobalization, on the other hand, is the equivalent of staying home and refusing to engage with others—it isolates nations and makes cooperation more difficult. If this inward focus also leads to breaking alliances, then democracies will struggle to defend themselves, and the cost of doing so will rise dramatically.

Additionally, alliances help countries spread out the risks, both economically and militarily. Withdrawing from alliances can lead to countries spending more on the military or to build up to a larger nuclear arsenal. Imagine living in a neighborhood with 100 houses, where the average home value is $500,000. Every year, one house tragically burns down. You have two options: either you save up $500,000 by yourself to cover the potential cost of rebuilding your house, or all 100 neighbors contribute $5000 each year to a shared fund. If the former is your only option, you will likely live in a smaller house, with some savings, just in case your house burns down. With the other option, if a house burns down, the fund pays for it, ensuring no single person bears the full financial burden alone, and everyone shares the risk equally. Alliances must be maintained, otherwise the fires might spread from house to house.

This same principle applies to disaster management within a country. FEMA, the US federal agency responsible for coordinating disaster relief, functions like the shared neighborhood fund—pooling resources from across the nation to help communities recover when disaster strikes. The second Trump Administration's plan to dismantle FEMA and leave disaster response up to individual states mirrors the "go it alone" approach. Without a centralized system, each state would be forced to shoulder the full financial and logistical burden of rebuilding after a disaster, leading to greater inequality in preparedness and response, and potentially allowing small-scale disasters to escalate into nationwide crises. We shall look at the power of alliances again when we come to discuss the economics of the *Grayzone*.

BIG GOVERNMENT

The fourth challenge to democracy is fiscal profligacy, another way of saying reckless government spending. This refers to the unsustainable cost of trying to level the playing field and reduce inequality by distributing money through programs that are not tied to work or merit.

Not long ago, a debt-to-GDP ratio of 60% was considered the upper limit for governments. This baseline percentage was even written into the Maastricht Treaty, which established the Euro. Today, however, debt levels are soaring. Italy is already at 130%, France is nearing 120%, and the US is on track to catch up. In fact, as of September 2024, the US's debt-to-GDP ratio reached 123.1%.[1] Only Germany has kept its ratio low, at 63%, thanks to a constitutional requirement.

Now we need to turn to some basic arithmetic. If a government spends money without generating a return—meaning the economy does not grow enough to cover the cost of borrowing—then debt will keep rising faster than GDP. It is like maxing out a credit card on things that do not increase income, such as luxury vacations or gadgets. Eventually, the debt piles up, and there is no source of income to help pay it off. It is the same when you borrow money at 10% and invest it at 5%. That is a losing strategy.

This is why debt-to-GDP ratios keep climbing—because the growing portion of the economy taken up by government spending is not producing enough returns to cover its costs. There may be very good reasons morally and socially to give out public transfers that do not generate growth equal to their cost, but the inevitable economic result will be to increase the debt to GDP. This is not inevitable though. We would argue that public investment and research and development can and should be made. They can generate permanent increases in productivity, growth, and jobs. But we will come to that later.

CONSEQUENCES

THE END OF THE CHINESE ECONOMIC MIRACLE

The fifth challenge to democracy is the end of China's economic miracle. Why is that? Shouldn't we celebrate the economic struggles of democracy's biggest rival? The answer is no—an economically unstable China may threaten us more, not less.

China's economic troubles stem from its reliance on two key drivers: the export of surplus production and the creation of bubbles. China's economy is now weighed down by excessive borrowing, property bubbles, and an unbalanced fiscal system. To keep things afloat, the government is pouring in massive amounts of money through stimulus packages. However, these measures are merely Band-Aids; they will not fix the self-inflicted wounds to the Chinese economy. China needs a surgical operation to create long-term growth and/or improve the economy's efficiency.

Another way to view the end of China's growth era is through its household savings surplus. With limited social services for education, healthcare, and retirement, families were forced to save heavily. As a result, private-sector savings often reached 40% of income in a typical year.

China's high household savings did not just sit idle—they were funneled into state-owned banks as deposits. These banks then lent the money to state-owned enterprises, property developers, and mortgage borrowers. However, the amount of consumer savings far exceeded what was needed to meet domestic demand. To make use of the surplus, China invested heavily in producing more goods for export. This led to a flood of cheap manufactured products that undercut competitors in wealthier nations, further fueling China's economic growth at the expense of other countries' manufacturing sectors.

This export-driven growth model, however, carried the seeds of its own collapse. Over time, excess investments were funneled into increasingly unproductive projects, causing the efficiency of China's capital to plummet.

China's industrial overcapacity has led to significant economic inefficiencies, with entire industries producing far more than market demand can absorb. In 2015, more than half of China's steel companies posted a loss as oversupply drove prices so low that steel was reportedly cheaper than cabbage.[2] This problem extends beyond steel. According to author Dinny McMahon, in *China's Great Wall of Debt*, China produces 13 times more aluminum than the US and accounts for about 50% of global supply, and while at its peak, it manufactured over 40% of the world's ships. According to Chinese state media, 21 industries suffer from "serious" overcapacity, including cement, power generation, solar panels, wind turbines, chemicals, and shipping.[3] These inefficiencies have created structural economic risks, as companies struggle with declining profitability, mounting debt, and wasted resources. This pattern underscores China's ongoing challenge of balancing industrial expansion with sustainable demand, a problem that reverberates through both its domestic economy and global markets.

Another example of China's investment inefficiencies is the widespread existence of ghost cities—massive urban developments that remain largely unoccupied. Researchers at Baidu, the Chinese equivalent of Google, identified at least 50 cities that fit that description across the country, highlighting the severe overcapacity in real estate. These underutilized developments represent billions of dollars in sunk costs, straining local governments and banks that financed their construction.[4] With demand failing to match supply, property values stagnate, debt burdens grow, and financial instability looms, making ghost cities a glaring example of China's misallocation of resources.

In simpler terms, the amount of GDP generated per unit of investment dropped sharply over the past decade. China's declining investment efficiency is like pouring more and more water into a leaky bucket: the effort keeps increasing, but less and less is being retained. As returns on these investments declined, the loans used to finance them became less viable, leading to mounting insolvency. This situation eventually reached a breaking point, especially for the state-owned banks, which had been converting surplus savings into risky, unsustainable loans.

China's massive trade surpluses, fueled by its high savings, were a major reason manufacturing jobs disappeared in wealthier democracies—they simply could not compete with China's low-cost production.

And so finally, the Western, the rich democratic countries have said, "No, we are not going to let you do this anymore," which is why there is a rising tide of protectionism against China.

Over the past decade, China's economy has experienced a gradual slowdown in growth. In the early 2010s, annual GDP growth rates were around 7–8%. However, by 2019, the growth rate had declined to approximately 6.0%. With some fluctuations with the pandemic and post-pandemic years, current World Bank projections for 2024, 2025, and 2026 estimate growth rates of 4.9%, 4.5%, and 4.0%, respectively.[5]

But what happens if China loses both its engine of export growth and its domestic growth fueled by heavy borrowing at the same time? This presents a challenge for democracies because no one knows how China will behave as its economic growth slows to 3% or less. And given its size and influence, China cannot be ignored.

Let us take a moment to reflect—democracy is remarkably resilient when faced with crises. However, it tends to be slow and inefficient at identifying problems and addressing them. In many respects it is a rear-view-mirror system.

Unlike democracies, autocracies operate through a top-down approach, making them much better at setting long-term goals and acting decisively. For example, they can prioritize industries like solar energy or electric vehicles early on and push them forward using state subsidies, often achieving rapid results that benefit society. However, autocracies are fragile. They lack the ability to correct mistakes because their leaders are often surrounded by loyalists and "yes men" rather than independent thinkers. Their legitimacy usually hinges on economic success, unless they resort to extreme measures like using force to maintain control. Ultimately, bad decisions in autocracies fall squarely on the leader, making the system particularly vulnerable.

Chinese President Xi Jinping's decade-long increasingly absolutist rule of China is a catalogue of economic errors, and the current economic crisis may be one too many.

When a giant tree falls in a forest you do not want to be picnicking underneath it. China is that tree. It is too big to fall silently, without sending shock waves through the forest. We, the democracies, have nowhere else to picnic but underneath it. Watch out!

The Chinese Communist Party holds power without public elections, deriving its legitimacy from consistent economic growth. Its survival hinges on improving living standards year after year and ensuring that each generation is wealthier than the last. If the Chinese government fails to uphold its economic promise, the social contract that legitimizes its rule will collapse. When that happens, it will not be the influence of wealthy democracies that destabilizes China—it will unravel from within.

Why does that affect and weaken us as democracies? It is because, as China becomes more unstable, it is possible that it will become more hostile and aggressive. This aligns with the political idea of "wag the dog," where a government might create external conflicts or escalate tensions to distract its population from domestic issues. In the case of China, increasing hostility toward democracies could serve as a diversion from internal instability, such as slowing economic growth or public dissatisfaction. Such hostilities would not only heighten global tensions but also force democracies to divert resources and attention away from internal progress to counter these manufactured external threats.

Nations are more likely to start external wars when their economies are declining rather than when they are growing. A historical example of this is Japan in the 1930s and 1940s. As its economy struggled during the Great Depression, Japan faced resource shortages and saw military expansion as a solution. To secure vital raw materials like oil, rubber, and metals, it launched aggressive campaigns across the Pacific, invading Manchuria in 1931, China in 1937, and eventually resource-rich nations in Southeast Asia and attacking the US at Pearl Harbor in 1941. This set of events demonstrates that how economic decline can push nations toward external conflicts as a means of securing resources and restoring national strength. European imperialism may be an exception, but this pattern is consistent with China's current ambitions. China's blueprint for a new world order and its territorial goals reflect a modern form of imperialism.

Think back to our earlier discussion about Taiwan and China. Taiwan, a free, democratic country with a thriving economy, would be a great addition to China's struggling economy. Taiwan remains the most likely flashpoint for a major conflict. China could begin by imposing a blockade against or, though less likely, launch a full-scale invasion of Taiwan. Such actions could also extend to the seizure of additional territory along the first and second island chains off China's eastern coast. This is a threat we must prepare for by strengthening our defenses, as well as addressing the economic dimensions of *Grayzone* warfare—a topic explored in detail later in this book.

Simply put, China poses a significant strategic challenge, whether its economy continues to grow or faces a crisis. Within a decade, its nuclear arsenal is expected to rival that of the US, creating the possibility of a dual-front threat with Russia. An unstable China, however, could present an even greater and less predictable dangers than its current efforts to economically outpace democracies and undermine the global order.

We will not debate whether democratic nations' defense spending should be 2% or 5% of GDP, or whether investments like building factories in Ukraine count as defense expenditures. Those decisions are best left to military economics experts. What is clear, however, is that military spending will need to at least double if China continues to weaken democracies. Two key factors drive this: first, reverting to isolationism is far more costly than maintaining mutual defense alliances; second, eroding trust among former allies could lead to a nuclear arms race, as nations seek to build their own systems of deterrence for self-preservation.

While military spending produces advanced equipment and technology, it does not significantly contribute to productivity, living standards, or wealth creation in the private sector. This is why economically struggling autocracies, especially those that are unstable and unpredictable, pose a serious threat to democracy.

Throughout the rest of this book, we will go into more detail about each of the most threatening challenges that democracies around the world are facing, and the potential consequences of autocracies taking over. Hopefully, after reading this book, you will come out understanding the gravity of the time we live in, and why it is such a pivotal turning point. Our intention is not to scare the reader, or to be overly pessimistic about the future of democracy, it is quite the opposite. We intend for each of you reading this to have a deeper understanding of how you can help combat these threats and preserve democracy for generations to come. Otherwise, the consequences could be dire.

CHAPTER THREE

POPULISM

First of all, let us define populism. Populism is a political movement that strives to appeal to ordinary people who feel that their concerns are being disregarded by established elite groups that control politics and the bureaucracy.

Populism is like a megaphone for frustration—a political approach designed to amplify the voices of those who feel ignored or sidelined by the perceived powerful elites who run governments and institutions. Imagine a crowded town hall where the regular folks at the back of the room suddenly get a microphone and start shouting their grievances. That is populism in essence: a way to cut through the noise of political bureaucracy and demand attention.

This idea is not new, but it has taken on a sharper edge in modern times. From the chants of "drain the swamp" in Washington to "gilets jaunes" (yellow vests) protests in Paris, populism emerges when people feel the system is easily manipulated. It is fueled by a sense of alienation and a deep distrust of elites who seem more interested in their own agendas than in serving the public. This disconnect creates fertile ground for leaders who promise to "restore power to the people"—whether they can deliver or not.

That is all well and good—it is nice to see people connecting again, but not in this manner. What is making this possible, though, is social media. Populism thrives on it, using social media platforms to spread ideas and spark conversations across a much broader audience than when we were limited to receiving our news from the local paper delivered to our residences. If something felt wrong back then, we would write a letter to the editor. When it was time to vote, we chose the party that seemed most aligned with fixing those issues. Today, though, social media has taken center stage—it is essentially the nervous system of populism, as we will explore in the next chapter.

HOW DID WE GET HERE?

As always, it is good to know how we got where we are, so a small bit of history will help. Let us take a brief look at the history of populism. The kind of populism we're discussing today—fueled by the internet—is relatively new.

However, there are other forms of populism in history. Consider the French Revolution in 1789 for example, when the monarchy was overthrown in a wave of public fervor. That could certainly be called a populist movement. But for now, we are focusing on the version of populism shaped by modern communication platforms, to which we all have access in the palm of our hands. After all, there were no emails, tweets, or TikToks from Marie Antoinette, Robespierre, or Louis XVI for the French citizens to consume and dissect. So, let us leave them out of this discussion for the moment.

Populism, as we know it today, gained traction globally after the fall of the Berlin Wall and the "end" of communism in 1989. Before then, most countries were led by centrist, elitist parties and politicians. The political center held firm because the looming threat on the other side of the wall demanded unity to protect our daily way of life. At this point in history, it was better to conform to protect one's bacon and eggs in the morning rather than to rock the boat and risk facing the shortages and stale bread that were the norm in the Soviet Union.

This shift was most noticeable in Europe, where the Cold War played out, compared to the Americas or Asia. Once the Cold War ended, there was no longer a pressing need to align with Christian Democrats or Social Democrats. People felt free to join niche parties—like a farmer's party or even a pro-mushroom-gathering party—without worrying that it would significantly impact their way of life.

Before the Berlin Wall fell, supporting parties that advocated for US withdrawal from Europe or the removal of nuclear weapons, placed individuals in a precarious position. Such stances often aligned with Soviet disinformation campaigns, making those who voiced them, knowingly or not, instruments of communist propaganda. In a time when ideological battles defined the Cold War, even well-meaning dissent could echo the narratives crafted in Moscow, casting doubt on their true intentions.

During this era, the West was gripped by the "Red Scare"—a pervasive fear of communist infiltration and espionage. Joining movements that undermined Western alliances was akin to poking holes in the very fabric of a secure, democratic way of life. It was the presence of NATO, American military forces, and nuclear deterrence that shielded Europe from Soviet influence and ensured the freedoms people relied upon. In a subtle way, supporting a non-centrist party was like being a mouse nibbling away at a block of cheese. You were unknowingly undermining the very way of life on which you depended—one safeguarded by nuclear deterrence, American forces, and NATO.

But once the threat disappeared, people felt free to say and do whatever they wanted, knowing it would not have much impact on their lives. This shift opened the door for new political parties and ideologies to emerge across

Europe. For example, green parties gained prominence, focusing on environmental issues that had been sidelined during the Cold War. Regionalist movements, like Catalonian independence in Spain or the Scottish National Party in the UK, also found a stronger footing. Meanwhile, more niche and unconventional parties, such as Italy's Five Star Movement or Germany's Pirate Party, catered to specific grievances or cultural shifts, signaling a newfound freedom in political expression. For instance, the number of political groups in the European Parliament increased from seven at the beginning of the 1979–1984 parliamentary term to ten at the start of the 1989–1994 term, reflecting the rise of new political movements during that period.[1] This was, and still is, the largest number of political groups ever to be simultaneously represented. Thus, another reason for populism's emergence: the decline of traditional political parties. People no longer felt a strong need for them, and this trend has not just continued—it has accelerated over time.

THE GERMAN EXAMPLE

Germany provides the most clear-cut example of the decline of support for traditional political parties, but there have been similar shifts in countries like France and Italy. In France, movements like the National Rally (formerly the National Front) have risen by capitalizing on anti-immigration and nationalist sentiment. Italy has seen the rise of populist forces such as the Five Star Movement and the League, which challenge the old political order. However, these movements have fluctuated in influence, often struggling with internal divisions or failing to maintain long-term dominance in government. We will focus on Germany because it could be the most extreme.

In Germany, the traditional center ground was historically dominated by a few key parties—the CDU (Christian Democrats), SPD (Social Democrats), and FDP (Liberals). These parties shared dominance over the political landscape well after the fall of the Berlin Wall, through coalitions and periods of unipolar control.

However, parties' influence wanes significantly in recent years as tensions have arisen in German society, particularly around issues like immigration. Wars and failed states triggered massive waves of migrants seeking better lives—a challenge not unique to Europe, but a global phenomenon. In 2022, Germany received approximately 669,000 new immigrants on a long-term or permanent basis, marking a 25% increase from the previous year.[2] This influx contributed to a broader trend in Europe, which saw its international migrant population rise to nearly 87 million in 2020, an increase of almost 16% since 2015.[3] Globally, the number of international migrants reached around 281 million in 2020, accounting for 3.6% of the world's population.[4]

The influx of newcomers left many Germans feeling threatened. Neighborhoods that were once entirely German became more diverse, sparking fears over job security and cultural change. Seeking protection, many turned away from traditional parties, which failed to address these concerns. When Angela Merkel, then Chancellor of Germany, opened the country's doors to immigration, she confidently stated, "Wir schaffen es"—"We can do it!" However, many Germans disagreed, feeling that their voices and anxieties were being ignored.

This tension highlights a broader challenge of assimilation. Immigrants often wish to preserve their cultural identity, maintaining their traditions, language, and way of life. At the same time, the host country seeks to foster a cohesive national identity, emphasizing shared values and unity. This clash can intensify feelings of alienation on both sides—newcomers may feel pressured to abandon their heritage, while native citizens may perceive a threat to their cultural fabric. In Germany, this struggle became particularly pronounced as Merkel's open-door policy tested the balance between inclusivity and integration, leaving many to question how a society can embrace diversity while preserving its own sense of self.

CONSEQUENCES

The influx of migrants into Germany has had multifaceted economic implications. On the one hand, the arrival of refugees has introduced a younger workforce, which is beneficial for a country facing an aging population and labor shortages in various sectors. Many migrants have filled essential roles, contributing to industries such as construction, healthcare, and information technology. For instance, in 2019, almost one in six people in skilled employment in Germany had not been born on German soil, highlighting the significant role of immigrants in the labor market.[5] However, integrating such a large number of newcomers has presented challenges. The rapid influx strained public services, including housing, education, and social welfare systems. Additionally, there have been concerns about higher unemployment rates among migrants compared to native Germans, indicating obstacles in effective integration into the workforce. These economic strains have fueled public debate and influenced political discourse, with some citizens feeling that resources are being stretched thin.

Public safety concerns have also intensified, particularly following incidents at public gatherings. In December 2024, a tragic event occurred at the Magdeburg Christmas market, where a vehicle was deliberately driven into the crowd by an immigrant, resulting in multiple fatalities and injuries. The attack led to increased anxiety among citizens, with many questioning the adequacy of security measures at public events. This incident, among others, has heightened the perception of vulnerability and has been a focal point in discussions about national security and immigration policies.

Many Germans began to feel that their country was being run by an out-of-touch elite that failed to represent ordinary citizens—a sentiment echoed in other nations like the US. This dissatisfaction led to the rise of the Alternative for Germany (AfD), a political party that initially formed to oppose the introduction of the euro. While the party was originally spearheaded by academics with unconventional economic ideas, the leadership was soon replaced by far-right figures promoting nationalist, anti-immigrant rhetoric, and fostering a divisive political climate. Some have even gone so far as to call these new party leaders "fascists."

The AfD promotes the policies you might expect, driven by the fears of everyday people—particularly the traditional German "Mittelstand," or middle class—who no longer felt secure in their once stable position. Feeling increasingly vulnerable, they turned to populism for answers.

In late 2024, around 20% of German voters supported the AfD. In the eastern states of Germany, this figure increased to a whopping 40%, where the AfD shares the political stage with an extreme left-wing party rooted in the former East German Communist Party. Both parties appeal to voters with anti-immigration and nationalist platforms, reflecting significant shifts in political allegiances. Even tech entrepreneur Elon Musk publicly endorsed the AfD; clearly, this new political movement is significant and cannot be ignored. However, other major parties have expressed an unwillingness to form coalitions with the AfD due to its right-wing, extremist ideologies, limiting its potential to govern.

So, why is this so important? The once-stable center of German politics—dominated by middle-class support for parties like the CDU, SPD, and FDP—has effectively collapsed. There is now a significant void in the political spectrum's middle ground, a hallmark of populism's disruptive impact.

Populism leads to a decline in traditional political parties, and populist parties are quick to step into the political void left behind. What truly fueled the rise of populist parties was the advent of technology and social media, a topic discussed in the next chapter.

Germany's traditional parties, which had dominated since 1945, were increasingly viewed as out of touch. They had become fat cats, while the middle class declined and became increasingly indigent. Many saw the traditional parties as corrupt, unresponsive, and more focused on serving vested interests than addressing the concerns of ordinary citizens.

Adding to this discontent was globalization, which caused many traditional jobs, particularly in manufacturing, to vanish. These were the roles often held by voters who once supported centrist parties, leaving them feeling abandoned and disenfranchised. The factory worker watched his job disappear as the company shifted manufacturing to China or India. At the same time, workers faced growing competition for unskilled jobs from migrants who had recently moved into the neighborhood. Frustrated, the factory worker is began to reconsider his voting stance.

This is noteworthy because the social dimension of skilled workers in Central Europe, particularly in Germany, Switzerland, and Holland, is not the same as in Anglo-Saxon countries.

Apprenticeships are the key to understanding this point. In those in Central European countries a mechanic, fitter, carpenter, or electrician served a long apprenticeship, usually sponsored by a corporation, before being qualified. The apprenticeship was a form of post-secondary education for those who did not pursue years of study to become professionals like engineers, economists, or architects, but instead chose to master practical, knowledge-intensive trades. An apprenticeship was considered equal to with a university education with respect to skills that were core to the manufacturing vocations which lay at the center of the German post-war economic miracle and core competence. More importantly, it held social status: the carpenter was "up there" with the eye doctor.

The collapse of German manufacturing disrupted far more than just an industrial sector. It dismantled a societal framework of respect and cohesion that had long been central to the nation's identity.

Globalization alone did not hollow out German manufacturing—domestic policy choices also played a significant role. Under Angela Merkel's leadership, Germany became heavily dependent on cheap Russian energy, a move that left the country vulnerable to geopolitical risks. For example, the Nord Stream gas pipelines, meant to secure energy flow from Russia, became a critical dependency that limited Germany's energy independence.

At the same time, Merkel prioritized maintaining German auto exports to China, despite the sector's lagging innovation. German carmakers, reliant on internal combustion engines, struggled to adapt to the global shift toward electric vehicles. China initially welcomed these exports, but within a decade, it had turned from a lucrative market into a formidable competitor. Chinese companies like BYD and Nio not only began dominating the electric vehicle market but also pushed German manufacturers into a corner, eroding their global market share.

The economic pressures from globalization and the collapse of manufacturing were not just financial in Germany—they tore at the social cohesion that had held communities together. Traditional middle-class pride, built on skilled trades and stable industries, gave way to frustration and insecurity. Populist parties capitalized on this turmoil, presenting themselves as the defenders of national identity and the protectors of those left behind by political elites and global competition.

DEMOCRACY vs POPULISM

To further understand this shift, let us look at the mechanics of populism—how populist parties are structured and how they function. It is difficult to fully explain their operations and architecture without using visuals, so a graphic will help illustrate these concepts more clearly.

There follows a visual representation comparing how political systems operate under traditional liberal democracy, which we will compare to populism. In a traditional liberal democracy, the structure resembles a pyramid. At the base are the people, holding a wide range of pluralistic and diverse views. These views are reflected in their support for an equally diverse set of political parties. During elections, people vote, and the outcome is typically the formation of a government—often a coalition. This process acts as a filtering system, distilling a variety of opinions into a cohesive governing framework.

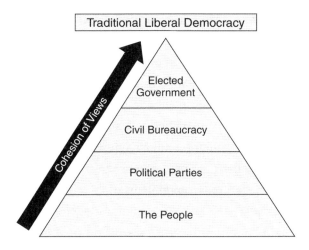

Individual opinions are homogenized into support for a party that might not reflect all their views but aligns with most or enough of them. Once elected, these parties also have to compromise and adjust their policies to work within a coalition government. In countries like the UK, where the first-past-the-post electoral system dominates, single-party rule is the norm, though these governments often include a range of viewpoints. It is no coincidence that the British coined the term "broad church," meaning an organization, group, or movement that serves as a middle ground for a wide range of opinions, beliefs, or approaches within its framework. In simple terms, it's a broad spectrum of the population and its beliefs.

The point about the whole process is that from top to bottom, it actually represents a system of harmonization, simplification, and condensation of views from the individual through the party to the elected party or parties, which then enact their policy for the period they are in office.

The process works much like a coffee filter. You place a paper filter into the cone-shaped insert, add ground coffee, and pour in boiling water. The water flows through, infusing with the coffee grounds to create the final brew in the pot. Imagine the coffee grounds as the millions of voters' opinions—diverse, scattered, and individual. The boiling water represents the voting process, pouring over these opinions to extract and refine them. As the water passes through the filter, it combines with the grounds, harmonizing the multitude of perspectives. What emerges in the pot is the final product: the elected government, a distilled and unified representation of the people's collective will. Just as the coffee filter ensures a smooth, drinkable brew, the traditional political system filters and condenses the variety of public opinions into cohesive policies and leadership.

During a government's term in office, there is little opportunity for public recourse, except in rare cases of major scandals or votes of confidence. For the most part, democracy operates indirectly with minimal input or consultation from the people.

This system of indirect democracy allows the ideas of the public to be transformed into the policies of the ruling parties. Once elected, these parties are left to govern without much interference and are largely unaffected by changes in voter opinion during their time in office.

Populism operates very differently. It divides society into supporters and opponents, with opponents labeled as the enemy. Supporters are viewed as a single, unified group, sharing the same perspectives as the populist party which claims to know and represent their views entirely.

Two relative truths emerge from this. The first truth is that communication between the party and its supporters is always direct, facilitated primarily by social media. The second vital aspect of populism is that it requires a common enemy, which could be immigrants, bureaucrats,

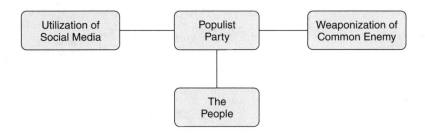

political elites, or foreign adversaries. There must always be something to hate and attack. As the song "You've Got to Be Carefully Taught" from the 1948 musical *South Pacific* poignantly observes, hatred and fear are not innate but are "drummed in your dear little ear" over time. Populism carefully cultivates this fear, teaching its followers "to hate all the people your relatives hate" and to distrust those "whose skin is a different shade." These lyrics capture the insidious way division is nurtured, turning manufactured enemies into the fuel that sustains populist movements.

Populism removes the need for compromise or filtering, as diverse views are dismissed as belonging to the enemy. The party positions itself as a unified entity that "knows" what its supporters want and directs them on whom or what to oppose. The traditional middle layer of the political process, which balances and integrates diverse opinions, is completely absent in populism. Those are the major differences.

HOW POPULISM WORKS

While populism could adopt central, consensus-driven ideas, this is rarely how it operates in practice. In fact, there is nothing in the structure of liberal democracies or populist systems that inherently prevents them from pursuing similar policies, so long as those policies have public support. However, that is not how things have played out.

One clear patter emerges from examining populist governments that have taken or approached power: they rely on identifying a common threat or enemy, a tactic that is not central to liberal democratic systems. Populist governments excel at discovering what ordinary people are most worried about, what their obsessions are. In most cases these voters are most concerned about economic insecurity, public safety, unwanted cultural changes, elitism/corruption, and living standards.

The best way to show how this might work is through a fictional example. Imagine a populist government, let us call it the Unity and Sovereignty Front (USF). The USF determines that the largest fear of the people in its country, Valtoria, is that they will lose their job and their living standard to immigrants or to globalization. Then the USF provides a common enemy, which is the cause of this anxiety among the people of Valtoria. It can be a racial enemy, or it can simply be an enemy like immigration in general, or it can be a faraway enemy like China.

This USF might target China as a common enemy, accusing it of flooding the market with cheap goods and threatening local jobs and industries. That might not be enough to stir up the people, so to intensify fear and hatred, the USF could claim that China is waging biological warfare by creating and spreading COVID-19. It might even weave in conspiracy theories, suggesting collaboration between China and domestic entities like a Valtorian intelligence agency, adding the "Deep State" into part of the narrative. This kind of propaganda creates a potent mix of fear and resentment, galvanizing the masses against a perceived external threat.

The USF then steps in with simplistic solutions and bold promises, presenting itself as the savior of the nation. It vows to tackle immigration, often through strict border controls, deportation policies, or even building physical barriers. It pledges to curb cheap imports by imposing tariffs, renegotiating trade deals, or promoting domestic industries under the banner of economic nationalism. These promises are packaged as quick fixes to restore jobs, protect cultural identity, and ensure economic stability, creating the illusion that such measures will solve all problems and lead to a prosperous and harmonious future.

The USF does not evaluate whether the fears fueling public anxieties, the chosen common enemy, or the proposed policies are based on rational arguments. Nor is there any genuine analysis of whether these policies can deliver the promised results. Instead, the populist leadership wins in elections and is handed unchecked power, as skepticism and critical thinking among their supporters are intentionally suppressed. There are several reasons for that: disinformation, "truth" created from lies, and the fact that of the support for populist parties often comes from people without tertiary education and from lower-income groups. This will be discussed further in the next chapter.

There are two key factors built into the populist model which require our attention.

The first key factor is that populist parties can never govern for the entire society or foster unity, because they need an antagonist. Populism thrives on having an internal enemy, which inherently makes its power divisive. To maintain control, populist governments often deepen polarization, which poses a serious threat to democracy. This division leaves a portion of the population feeling alienated and viewing democracy itself as an adversary.

This explains why some populist leaders openly admire dictators. Leaders like Hungary's Viktor Orbán cozying up to Vladimir Putin, or America praising autocratic rulers, may seem baffling at first glance. But these displays are not about practical benefits to their nations. Instead, they send a message to their supporters: autocracies are not the enemy—they are allies. This subtle normalization of authoritarianism weakens faith in democracy and gives populist leaders more freedom to erode democratic systems at home.

The second key factor in populist regimes is that the people they appoint to positions of power. These appointees are chosen not for their competence but for their loyalty to the party or its leader. They deeply believe in the "righteousness" of their cause, often at the expense of critical thinking. This loyalty-first approach means they lack the skills to analyze, adapt, or even question the policies they are tasked with implementing.

Vladimir Putin's rise from a relatively unknown figure to prime minister and eventually President of Russia illustrates this dynamic. Initially a mid-level KGB officer and later a deputy mayor of St. Petersburg, Putin was handpicked by Boris Yeltsin and his inner circle, not for his track record of reform but for his perceived loyalty and reliability. Once in power, Putin strategically surrounded himself with loyalists—many from his old KGB network—who prioritized allegiance over competence, enabling him to consolidate power and silence dissent.

Nicolás Maduro's tenure in Venezuela is another example. Following Hugo Chávez's death, Maduro, a former bus driver and union leader with limited experience in governance, was chosen as Chávez's successor due to his unwavering loyalty to the socialist regime. Once in power, Maduro appointed a cadre of similarly unqualified but loyal allies to key positions. Their inability to address Venezuela's spiraling economic crisis only deepened the country's turmoil, demonstrating how loyalty-driven appointments can destabilize a nation.

This is why some populist parties target the professional bureaucracy, labeling it as the "Deep State." Their goal is to dismantle it and replace it with loyal party members. By doing so, they eliminate a key part of the democratic system—the checks and balances that expose flawed or harmful policies. Few things pose a greater threat to democracy than this deliberate erosion of accountability.

This is also why populists often aim to undermine judicial independence. An impartial judiciary provides a critical check on the abuse of power, something populist leaders find inconvenient. Their solution? Pack the courts with loyalists who will prioritize the party's agenda over justice. For example, since 2010, Orbán's government in Hungary has systematically weakened democratic institutions by amending the constitution, undermining judicial independence, and stacking the Constitutional Court with loyalists. These actions have concentrated power within the ruling Fidesz party, eroding checks and balances essential to a democratic system.[6]

You might ask, what happens when the populists implement all these policies like immigration and tariffs, but they do not work? Will they not be voted out? Is that not the ultimate check on the exercise of power?

In the US, for example, populist politicians might lose power temporarily, but manage to get re-elected, even when their policies fall short. On the other hand, most European countries have resisted electing populist leaders, though there are exceptions like Italy. The Brothers of Italy party gained power by toning down many of its extreme populist positions and focusing on pragmatic economic policies. However, the Meloni government still holds strong anti-immigration views, seeking to deport migrants to countries like Albania or, in the UK's case, to Rwanda. Over time, though, the realities of governing tend to soften some of the harsher edges of populism.

In the US, a populist government that lost a second election was ultimately able to get reelected on a nearly identical platform of tariffs, immigration reform, and tax cuts. How is that possible if, during its first term of office, its policies did not produce the desired effects? If the same polices are needed, doesn't this prove they did not work the last time?

The answer lies in the powerful grip populist ideas have on their supporters. These ideas are ingrained so deeply that even when populist policies fail, voters continue to believe they are the right solutions. This persistence stems from fears and insecurities left unresolved, either by ineffective policy or exaggerated issues.

Why do these beliefs remain unshaken, even when the policies fail to deliver results. We will discuss this in our chapter on discourse.

POPULISTS IN THE REAL WORLD

The continuing rise of populists is far from guaranteed. In 2024, they were ousted in Poland through democratic elections and failed to gain control in the EU Parliament, Belgium, and the Netherlands. In Hungary, Viktor Orbán's questionable dealings might soon cost him power. However, populists are poised to win in France and possibly Spain, and they have already secured leadership in Slovakia. In Germany, the AfD made history by voting alongside the center-right CDU for the first time to pass a parliamentary motion aimed at significantly restricting migration. This move broke a longstanding post-war taboo against cooperation with the far right and has sparked significant controversy. This mixed trajectory highlights a critical pattern: while populists thrive in environments of economic frustration, political polarization, or perceived elitism, their hold on power can be fragile. When voters see tangible failures or corruption, they can and do push back, reminding us that democracy, even when weakened, retains the power to correct course.

Populists are most dangerous when they align with the forces of autocracy, leveraging powerful propaganda and disinformation-spreading techniques and external funding to amplify their influence and manipulate elections. Such an alliance not only undermines democracy but also emboldens authoritarian regimes worldwide. As we close this chapter, it is clear that populism, while a powerful force, is neither inevitable nor invincible. Its rise and fall depend on the resilience of democratic institutions and the vigilance of informed citizens.

CHAPTER FOUR

SOCIAL MEDIA AND THE NETWORK EFFECT

P opulism has not risen in a vacuum. Its explosive growth across the globe is tightly interwoven with the rapid expansion of social media. Understanding either phenomenon requires understanding the other. To grasp how populist movements gain momentum and influence millions, one must first explore how collective behavior operates in the natural world.

COLLECTIVE BEHAVIOR

Imagine a shimmering school of sardines gliding through the ocean, twisting and turning in perfect harmony. This is not just a display of nature's elegance—it is a survival strategy powered by collective decision-making.

You will notice one thing immediately when watching these fish. They always stick together. If they go in any direction, they all go together. How do they know how to do this?

Imagine an experiment where two food sources are placed in the water—one at the top and one at the bottom, below a school of fish. The fish will swim toward the middle, the gap between those two food sources, and then suddenly, in an instant, they will decide, and will all swim together toward the single food source. How is that decision made?

To find out, researchers attached tiny electrodes to the brains of these fish to study how they make decisions. As the fish get closer to the point where they must choose between the two food sources, certain neurons in their brains begin to activate. Not every fish's brain shows this activity, but many do. Remarkably, the same neurons in the same brain regions light up across different fish.[1] This shared brain activity sends a clear signal, guiding the entire group to turn in the same direction at the same moment. Essentially, the fish are connected through an internal network, allowing them to communicate and make decisions as a group. This network directly shapes the path they choose to follow.

Much like these fish, human societies have become deeply interconnected through digital networks. The forces that guide those sardines mirror the social forces guiding modern political discourse. And just like that, the path from fish to Facebook does not seem so far-fetched.

Now, let us shift from fish to a troop of baboons. Picture a group of males, females, and their young. Among them is a dominant male—the largest and strongest—who seems to rule the group. Picture the baboons sitting at a water hole, and deciding they are hungry for their next meal. Traditionally, it was believed that the alpha male called all the shots and decided where the troop goes next. If another baboon disagreed, the dominant male could simply assert his authority, perhaps with a swat or a growl, forcing the group to follow his lead.

However, research into baboon behavior tells a different story. By studying brain activity, scientists have discovered that decisions about where to move next are not made solely by the alpha male. Instead, the entire group participates in the decision-making process. Neurons in the brains of every member—whether it is the smallest, weakest female or the powerful alpha male—light up in the same way when the group is deciding where to go. This shared brain activity signals a consensus, guiding the whole troop toward a common direction.

Of course, baboons have more ways to communicate than fish. They use vocal sounds, gestures, and even facial expressions. Yet, just like the fish, their decisions are driven by synchronized brain activity. Once the group arrives at the next food source, the dominant male may use his strength to claim the best portions. But that does not mean he chose the destination. The choice was made collectively. Every member of the troop had a say in the journey.

This brings us back to human behavior, and why this animal behavior is so important to understand. Like fish and baboons, people are heavily influenced by the social context around them. Our perceptions and judgments often shift based on the company we keep. The ideas, opinions, likes, and dislikes of the people around us shape our own realities and affect what we believe to be true.

Consider a psychological experiment where an average-looking man was placed in a room with two different types of women. In scenario one, he stood alone or alongside an average-looking woman. In scenario two, he was paired with a woman considered more attractive by society's standards.

Participants—both men and women—were then asked to rate everybody taking part in the experiment in terms of their relative attractiveness (physical, personality, and so on). The results were clear: when the man was alone or paired with an average woman, he was seen as just that—average. But when he stood beside a more attractive woman, people rated him as more appealing, and other women in the room began to take an interest in him. These dynamics sparked competition among the other women for the average man's attention—especially if the attractive woman continued to stay by his side.[2] This phenomenon is known as mate-choice copying, and it demonstrates how the perceived value of something, in this case a potential partner, can be altered by the opinion of others.

This is an example of how group behavior can create social norms and directly influence individual actions. In social settings, people often look to others for cues on how to think, feel, and act—a phenomenon known as *social proof*. When others show interest in someone or something, it signals value, making that person or object more desirable. This effect does not just shape romantic interest; it drives trends in fashion, technology, and even politics.

For instance, a product that suddenly becomes popular on social media or the celebrity endorsement often experiences a surge in sales, not necessarily because it is superior, but because people assume that widespread popularity must indicate quality. Similarly, political movements gain momentum when large groups rally behind them, making others more likely to join simply because the crowd's enthusiasm signals legitimacy.

In today's digital world, anyone with a large following can become an "influencer," using that status either to spread valuable knowledge or to serve their own interests. Social media has flattened traditional hierarchies of knowledge, allowing popularity to be mistaken for authority. A well-timed tweet or viral video can shape opinions, drive political movements, or sell products—not because the information is necessarily true or valuable, but because we instinctively assign credibility to those with the biggest audiences and the most likes. In this way, the power to influence has become democratized, but also has the risk of misinformation spreading unchecked.

This subtle pressure to follow group behavior influences our choices in ways we often do not recognize, shaping societal norms and guiding collective decisions.

HYPERCONNECTED AND HYPERPOLARIZED

Now, let us turn our attention to social media. Don't worry—this is not going to be a history lesson on how the internet was invented or how platforms like Facebook, Twitter, and TikTok came into existence. By now, we are all living in the digital age, so let us just accept that social media is deeply woven into our daily lives and moving forward.

What truly matters is understanding how social media has completely transformed the way information spreads, both in terms of distance and speed. Ideas, opinions, and news no longer stay within small, local communities. Instead, they cross borders, languages, and cultures in an instant. What was once a conversation shared over a dinner table can now become a global discussion within seconds. A single tweet or video can reach millions, influencing minds and sparking movements.

Think about viral campaigns like the *Ice Bucket Challenge*, a trend in which participants pour a bucket of ice water on themselves to spread awareness and raised millions for ALS research, or social movements like *#MeToo* and *Black Lives Matter*, which gained momentum through shared stories and videos. These examples show how social media can amplify voices that might otherwise go unheard. But this massive reach is not always positive—false information and harmful ideas can spread just as quickly.

That is the main difference between the 21st century and the decades prior. Information no longer flows from traditional, authoritative sources like newspaper editors, universities, research institutions, or trusted broadcasters such as the BBC—organizations once known for upholding high standards of accuracy and accountability.

Today, information spreads freely and casually between individuals, with little thought or verification—much like tossing a shoe at a noisy cat in the middle of the night, which will react without pause or consideration.

This change in how information spreads is crucial to understand; today's information landscape is completely flat. In the past, it functioned more like a well-structured liberal democracy—layered and organized. Let us use a coffee filter once again to explain what we mean. New information had to pass through filters, much like hot water passes through a coffee filter. There was a hierarchy involved in the distribution of information, whose function was to make it "responsible." The filter—trusted editors, fact-checkers, and reputable institutions—caught the grounds of misinformation and bias, allowing only clean, verified facts to flow through.

Now, that filter is gone. Information is poured directly into our cups—raw, unfiltered, and often bitter. Without that layer of careful review, rumors, falsehoods, and half-truths blend seamlessly with facts, making it harder than ever to tell what is true.

This filtering process was not limited to academic or official reports. It applied to journalism too. Before any news story reached the public, it underwent careful editing. Editors verified facts, cross-checked details with multiple sources, and ensured the information was accurate and reliable. Only after passing through this rigorous process would the story be published and shared with readers. Now, that is gone.

In *The World Is Flat*, Thomas Friedman explores how globalization has leveled the global playing field, allowing individuals, companies, and countries to connect and compete like never before. Advances in technology, from the internet to logistics systems, have "flattened" barriers, creating a world where geographic and economic boundaries are less relevant. Similarly, the flow of information has undergone a transformation. Where once knowledge was controlled by gatekeepers—publishers, media conglomerates, and academic institutions—it now moves freely across a digital landscape. Social media, search engines, and online platforms have flattened the information hierarchy, making it possible for anyone to share, access, and shape public discourse.

Today, information spreads wider, moves faster, and often undergoes no fact-checking. This combination has completely transformed the very nature of information—turning it from something carefully curated into something immediate, overwhelming, and often unreliable.

Those are not the only differences though. In the past, much of the information people shared came through face-to-face conversations. Trust was built on personal relationships—people needed to know and trust each other before accepting something as fact. Of course, rumors and gossip still existed, but within close-knit communities it was easier to recognize who tended to exaggerate or spread false information. Whether in a small village or an exclusive club of bankers and politicians, people naturally adjusted how much they trusted information based on who was sharing it.

That personal layer of trust is gone. Today, we may have profile pictures on websites or verified badges on social media, but that is not the same as knowing someone face-to-face. A blue checkmark on Twitter (X) or a verified account on Meta does not reveal a person's true character or credibility the way personal reputation once did.

On top of that, the anonymity offered by the internet has further eroded accountability. Online, people can hide behind fake names and anonymous profiles, giving them the freedom to spread misinformation, hate speech, and extreme opinions without fear of consequences. This shield of anonymity emboldens individuals to say things they would never dare express in person. It allows harmful ideas to circulate unchecked, fueling division and radicalization while protecting the people responsible from social or legal repercussions. This lack of accountability has created an environment where falsehoods and hostility can thrive.

When the internet first exploded in popularity, many believed it would help make rigid political systems more democratic. The hope was that leaders would become more accountable, as citizens could voice their concerns instantly—without having to wait for elections to express dissatisfaction.

But that vision of a more democratic world did not materialize. Information became diluted and distorted, overwhelmed by sheer volume, hijacked by extremists, and spread without fact-checking or trusted sources.

Also, the question of who controls these platforms has a major influence on these information highways. When powerful individuals or corporations control the channels of communication, they can use those channels to serve their own interests. Instead of promoting democracy, these platforms can be twisted into tools for manipulation and control. Take a look at some of the people who sat in the front row at President Trump's inauguration in 2025—Elon Musk and Mark Zuckerberg, owners of two of the largest and most used social media conglomerates in the world.

This issue is only further compounded by how social media adds another layer of confusion to the information we consume and the decisions we make. It can blur the line between fact and fiction, making it harder to recognize what is true and influencing how we think and act.

ECHO CHAMBERS AND AMPLIFICATIONS

One striking reality about the internet is that good news spreads slowly, while bad news travels fast. Negative stories, scandals, and alarming headlines grab attention and circulate rapidly, overshadowing positive or uplifting information. As a result, bad news has a much stronger impact on people's emotions and beliefs than good news ever could.

When it comes to beliefs, social media empowers lies to be presented as facts. For example, a wild rumor that your neighbor is eating your cat would likely go viral online, attracting thousands of clicks and shares—far more than a simple, heartwarming story about your neighbor adopting a kitten. If the lies are repeated often enough, they will become truth in the sense that people believe them to be true, even if they are not. The more "shares," "comments," and "likes" the story gets, the harder it becomes to dispel the story that began as a wild rumor.

You do not have to look far to find a prime example of such an instance, like during a 2024 presidential debate when President Donald Trump claimed, "In Springfield, they (Haitian immigrants) are eating the dogs. The people that came in, they are eating the cats. They're eating—they are eating the pets of the people that live there."[3] This baseless statement quickly ignited social media, with millions of users sharing and discussing the claim. The situation escalated when misleading videos began circulating online, supposedly showing Haitian migrants in Ohio engaging in this behavior. These videos were either heavily edited or taken out of context, but their graphic nature made them go viral. For days, it was difficult to debunk these clips because they spread faster than fact-checkers could respond. By the time reliable sources disproved the content, the false narrative had already solidified in the minds of many. This incident demonstrates how sensational lies, especially when amplified by influential figures and paired with misleading visuals, can overwhelm truth and fuel fear and division.

This rapid spread of misinformation is dangerous because social media has the power to turn false beliefs into real-world actions. Once people accept these fabricated stories as truth, they are more likely to act on them—sometimes in harmful or violent ways. Research shows that calls to action on social media are far more effective at driving immediate, physical responses than traditional forms of communication. In the case of the false claims about immigrants, social media did not just fuel online outrage—it encouraged real-life hostility and deepened societal divisions. The speed and reach of these platforms can convert dangerous ideas into dangerous behaviors almost instantly. This makes social media a powerful tool for spreading misinformation and inciting harmful behavior, as people are more likely to act on false or emotionally charged information before stopping to question its accuracy. For example, in 2020, false claims about the Coronavirus which spread rapidly online led to attacks on innocent people of Asian descent.

The January 6th insurrection at the US Capitol is an even more stark example of how social media can rapidly mobilize people to take dangerous, real-world action. In the weeks leading up to the attack, platforms like Twitter, Facebook, and Parler were flooded with false claims that the 2020 presidential election had been stolen. Hashtags such as #StopTheSteal and viral posts spread conspiracy theories, alleging widespread voter fraud without any credible evidence.

These lies did not just stay online—they turned into real-world plans. Encrypted messaging apps and fringe social media sites became echo chambers where users openly discussed storming the Capitol. Posts shared detailed maps of the Capitol building, advised on what gear to bring, and coordinated meeting points. Some even called for violence against lawmakers.

One notable example was a viral Facebook event titled *Stop the Steal Rally,* which attracted thousands of users. Parler, an alternative, right-wing social media platform, became a hub for more extreme content, with users sharing explicit threats and tactics for breaching security barriers. Videos and live streams from the day of the attack showed rioters using strategies that had been openly discussed online, including how to break windows and bypass police barricades.

The sheer speed and volume of misinformation allowed these ideas to spread unchecked, creating a sense of urgency and justification for violent action. Social media did not just amplify these falsehoods—it helped organize, encourage, and ultimately turn them into a coordinated assault on democracy.

. This example and countless others show us that repeated lies on social media can eventually be accepted as truth. This cycle of repetition is the foundation of fake news and conspiracy theories, allowing false narratives to take hold and influence public opinion. Over time, these distortions blur the line between fact and fiction, making it harder for people to distinguish reality from misinformation.

You might think that when people are shown clear evidence that something they believe is false, they will change their minds. But that is not always the case; it depends on where on the political spectrum the individual lies. Research shows that people with moderate political views—whether liberal, conservative, or social democratic—are more likely to update their beliefs when presented with new facts. However, those with extreme political views often react differently. When a false belief has been repeated enough to seem true, even solid evidence will not change their minds. In fact, the more proof they see that contradicts their belief, the more strongly they may cling to it.

This leads us to a critical realization: social media has not strengthened democracy—it has actively weakened it. The speed and reach of these platforms have allowed lies to be repeated so often that they start to feel like the truth, even when solid evidence proves otherwise. Social media algorithms, designed to promote content that will spur engagement, often show users the type of content they already agree with, creating more polarization and reinforcing false ideas. The saying "seeing is believing" has flipped into "believing is seeing," where people bend reality to fit their beliefs. Once a false idea takes hold, every new experience or piece of information is twisted to support that belief. Even visits to Auschwitz do not make Holocaust deniers change their mind; they will be quick to say that there are no bodies.

CONSEQUENCES

SOCIAL MEDIA AND POPULISM

This distorted way of thinking directly feeds into populism. Social media both reflects and fuels populist movements. It mirrors populism by breaking down traditional layers of communication and governance, allowing leaders to bypass checks and controls and speak directly to their followers. At the same time, it energizes populism by dividing societies and creating shared enemies, turning followers into active participants who can be easily mobilized.

A real-world example of this is the persecution of the Rohingya Muslim minority in Myanmar. In 2017, the Myanmar military launched a brutal campaign against the Rohingya, leading to thousands of deaths and forcing over 700,000 to flee the country.[4] But what led to this?

Myanmar, formerly known as Burma, opened itself to widespread international trade in 2010. Through globalization, Myanmar began to import cell phones, and the internet adoption rate of the Myanmar population jumped from 0.5% in 2010 to 40% in 2016.[5] To gain new users from this emerging market, Facebook made deals with phone providers all over the country, so that all phones sold came with Facebook pre-installed. Thus, this new dominant social media platform in Myanmar played a significant role in this crisis. In fact, about 38% of the population said that Facebook was their primary source of news.[6] The military and nationalist groups, such as the Buddhist 969 movement, used Facebook to disseminate anti-Rohingya propaganda, spreading false information that dehumanized the Rohingya and incited hatred. For example, posts falsely accused the Rohingya of plotting to overtake the country, leading to widespread fear and anger among the Buddhist majority.[7]

Facebook's algorithms, designed to promote engaging content, inadvertently amplified this harmful material. As users interacted with inflammatory posts, Facebook's systems prioritized similar content, creating echo chambers that intensified anti-Rohingya sentiments. Despite warnings from human rights organizations, Facebook failed to implement adequate measures to curb the spread of hate speech and disinformation.

This unchecked spread of false information led to real-world violence, which some have called an ethnic cleansing. "In the months and years leading up to the atrocities, Facebook's algorithms were intensifying a storm of hatred against the Rohingya which contributed to real-world violence," said Agnès Callamard, Amnesty International's Secretary General.[8] Misinformation on Facebook fueled public support for the military's actions, leading to widespread atrocities against the Rohingya, including killings, sexual violence, and the burning of villages.[9] The United Nations and Amnesty International have criticized Facebook for its role in facilitating these human rights abuses.[10] This case illustrates how social media platforms, when misused, can become tools for spreading disinformation and inciting violence, especially when there is a lack of effective moderation and accountability.

This is simply propaganda in a modern form. As chess grandmaster and political activist Garry Kasparov explains, "The point of modern propaganda is not only to misinform or push an agenda. It is to exhaust your critical thinking and to annihilate truth." In other words, the goal is not just to spread lies—it is to overwhelm people with so much false or confusing information that they stop questioning it altogether.

While propaganda easily captures those already convinced, its more dangerous impact targets the undecided. Political philosopher Hannah Arendt warned that the purpose of constant lying is not just to spread falsehoods but to destroy the very idea of truth. She explained that when people can no longer tell the difference between truth and lies, they also lose the ability to distinguish right from wrong. Over time, this confusion strips people of the power to think critically and make sound judgments. To paraphrase Arendt, a people that can no longer distinguish between truth and lies cannot distinguish between right and wrong. And such a people, deprived of the power to think and judge, is, without knowing and unwittingly willing to do it, completely subjected to the rule of lies. With such people you can do whatever you want. In this state, society becomes dangerously easy to manipulate and control. Put another way, if you don't have the knowledge or ability to think for yourself, someone else will think for you.

Populists on social media aim to create apathy among those who oppose them. By overwhelming people with misinformation and constant conflict, they wear down their critics, causing them to disengage. This lack of involvement weakens the democratic system because the individuals and institutions meant to hold leaders accountable lose the motivation to act. When watchdogs and concerned citizens give up, it becomes much easier for populists to erode democratic checks and balances.

We have not fully reached that point yet, but it is hard to ignore the warning signs. For instance, former President Trump suggested on multiple occasions that the 2020 election was not a fair election due to mail-in ballots—a statement that raised serious concerns about the future of democratic processes. Comments like this fuel distrust in elections and push democratic institutions closer to the brink.

SOCIAL MEDIA AS A WEAPON

Populists are not the only ones exploiting social media for their own gain. In many cases, they become unwitting tools for the *Axis of Autocracies*—which uses both populist-driven social media and its own disinformation campaigns to weaken democratic systems. These regimes skillfully spread false narratives and propaganda online to divide societies and erode trust in democratic institutions.

China, Russia, and Iran fully recognize that unrestricted access to social media is a major vulnerability in democratic societies. They understand how open platforms can be exploited to spread disinformation and sow division. As a result, these regimes tightly control social media within their own countries, censoring content and restricting free speech to prevent the same kind of disruption from threatening their own power.

In fact, it is more than just a small weakness, it is a wide-open gateway. The *Axis of Autocracies*, led by countries like China and Russia, actively exploits this opening to flood democratic societies with disinformation. The goal is to manipulate public opinion and weaken resistance to their own narratives, making people more susceptible to Chinese and Russian influence. There is confirmed evidence that Russia, China, and Iran have all launched disinformation campaigns to interfere in US elections. These countries have used social media and other online platforms to spread false information and deepen political divisions. In response, the US has used sanctions on individuals and organizations from these nations involved in these efforts, aiming to hold them accountable for trying to undermine American democracy.

In the ongoing struggle between democratic and authoritarian regimes, disinformation has become as powerful a weapon as guns, bombs, or bullets. This form of *Grayzone* warfare allows autocracies to weaken democracies from within, without ever firing a shot. The successes of Russian and Chinese efforts to align with local populist movements is the clearest measure of how effective their strategies are in undermining democracy. By supporting and amplifying these movements, they steadily erode democratic institutions and sow division within societies.

One example is in Slovakia, where Russian funding helped Robert Fico and his political allies win an election. His government is now known for having a high number of convicted and suspected criminals. One of Fico's first actions in office was to halt aid to Ukraine.[11] Shortly after, he traveled to Moscow to show support for Vladimir Putin—likely as a gesture of gratitude for Russia's backing. Notably, in August 2024, the government disbanded the National Crime Agency (NAKA), a key body responsible for investigating serious crimes, including political corruption. This action freed Peter Kažimír, the governor of Slovakia's central bank and former finance minister under Fico, who was charged with bribery, and the former special prosecutor, Dušan Kováčik, who was convicted for accepting bribes and leaking information about investigations. In an interview with *Politico*, former Prime Minister Ľudovít Ódor said, "The priority for [Fico] is to buy impunity for cronies, dismantle democracy, and set up some kind of autocratic regime."[12]

A more extreme example took place in Georgia. Russian interference in the October 26, 2024, parliamentary election helped the pro-Moscow Georgian Dream party and its leader, oligarch Bidzina Ivanishvili, stay in power. The manipulation was so severe that both Georgia's president, Salome Zourabichvili, and the European Parliament declared the election invalid. One of the Georgian Dream party's first moves was to suspend talks to join the EU until 2028—even though 80% of Georgians support EU membership.

In response, Georgia's president and courageous citizens took to the streets in Tbilisi, demanding new elections. Their peaceful protests were met with harsh repression and violence. The country's Supreme Court ruled the disputed election results as valid, with not a single judge daring to oppose the decision.

It now seems likely that Georgia has been effectively lost from democratic influence. Understanding the history behind this situation helps to explain how it unfolded.

In 2008, Russia invaded Georgia and seized control of the regions of Abkhazia and South Ossetia. This aggressive move served as a model for Russia's later invasion of Crimea in 2014. At the time, democracies were not as well aligned as they are today, and Western nations largely stood by without taking meaningful action to stop Russia. Major democracies like Germany, led by Chancellor Angela Merkel, remained silent as they deepened economic ties with Russia. Germany proceeded with the Nord Stream 2 pipeline project, increasing Europe's dependence on Russian natural gas and ignoring the growing threat posed by Moscow's aggression.

This lack of resistance likely contributed to Putin's belief that he could easily seize Ukraine without facing serious consequences from the West. Although he miscalculated that assumption, it did not change the *Axis of Autocracies*' core belief that democracy is weak and corrupt. In fact, the way democracies responded to the war only strengthened that perception.

Looking back to Georgia, the situation is grim. Russia is confident that democratic nations will not intervene to stop its takeover. Since the 2008 invasion, Russian intelligence agencies like the FSB and GRU have spent 16 years infiltrating and corrupting Georgia's democratic institutions, including the Supreme Court.

Russia attempted the same strategy in Moldova and Romania, but the outcome was different. Romania, as a successful member of the EU, proved more resilient, but Russia still came dangerously close to succeeding in its efforts to destabilize both countries.

In Moldova, two critical votes took place on October 20, 2024: a referendum to amend the constitution to support joining the EU and a presidential election. The pro-EU incumbent, President Maia Sandu, narrowly defeated the pro-Russian candidate, Alexandr Stoianoglo of the PSRM party. This close result was largely due to alleged widespread Russian interference, including vote buying, mass disinformation campaigns on social media, and ballot stuffing in pro-Russian regions like Transnistria. The interference was so severe that in June 2024, the US, UK, and Canada issued a joint statement condemning Russia's efforts to influence Moldova's election. Fortunately, despite these obstacles, Maia Sandu secured victory.

Romania stands out as one of the most blatant cases of election interference by the *Axis of Autocracies*. This time, both Russian and Chinese forces worked together to influence the outcome. They heavily used TikTok to boost Calin Georgescu, a little-known right-wing populist, helping him win the first round of the presidential election against the sitting prime minister, Marcel Ciolacu of the Social Democratic Party. Georgescu's popularity increased from 1% to 22% practically overnight, despite him claiming to spend no money on his campaign.[13] Georgescu's extreme policies include banning foreign investment in Ukraine and calling Ukraine a "fake" state while pushing to end support for it. Although Russia has denied any interference, Romania's intelligence service believes they played a role in cyberattacks, the creation of fraudulent accounts, false representation of the Romanian government, and paid for promotion on TikTok.

What might have been most eye-opening in this election was how quickly Calin Georgescu's TikTok account gained massive popularity. Practically overnight, his account skyrocketed to 52 million views per week leading up to the first round of voting. This sudden success was not organic—it was driven by hundreds of Russian-run fake social media accounts that spread false information and boosted his image. Funding such a massive disinformation campaign required significant money, and there is little doubt that it was supplied by foreign backers in the *Axis of Autocracies*.

However, Romania's civic institutions were much stronger and less influenced by the *Axis of Autocracies* compared to Georgia. After thoroughly reviewing the election process and results, Romania's Supreme Court annulled the election due to the widespread fraud. Soon after the ruling, several pro-Russian politicians were seen fleeing the country, heading to Dubai.

Shifting the focus back to Ukraine, one of Putin's greatest successes in the war was forcing Western nations to fight on his terms. His repeated threats of escalation, especially nuclear threats, caused global leaders to hesitate. Out of concern, leaders like President Biden and Chancellor Scholz held back from giving Ukraine the full military support it needed to win. The aid given has only prolonged the war. It is important to remember that Ukraine was not just defending its own country but also standing up for democratic values worldwide. If Russia wins, it could extend its influence into the EU within 5 years. Yet, Western governments bought into Putin's narrative and only provided Ukraine with limited aid, careful not to provoke him. But Putin was unlikely to use nuclear weapons—he knows that any such move would bring devastating consequences and leave him with nowhere to hide.

Putin's disinformation campaign was convincing people that democracies should limit their support for Ukraine. He also spread the false narrative that NATO was somehow responsible for Russia's unprovoked invasion. This misleading story shifted blame away from Russia and created doubt about the role of Western alliances in defending democracy.

Populist social media channels played a major role in supporting Putin's agenda. The individuals and groups spreading these messages actively helped promote his disinformation, betraying democratic values. Even today, some of these false narratives continue to be echoed by politicians running for high office. With allies undermining it from within, democracy does not need external enemies; it is at risk of collapsing on its own.

Russia's economy, in terms of GDP, is comparable in size to Italy's, and according to the IMF's October 2024 World Economic Outlook, Russia's nominal GDP at the time of writing is approximately $2.2 trillion, while Italy's is around $2.46 trillion.[14] However, Russia's ability to destabilize democracies far exceeds its economic strength. This imbalance highlights how the *Axis of Autocracies* excels at efficiently using its resources to undermine democratic systems. In contrast, democracies, despite their wealth, have been slow and complacent in defending themselves effectively.

As Chinese President Xi Jinping has suggested, democracies' complacency is their greatest weakness.

Democracy is not crumbling from a single blow—it is being quietly eroded, piece by piece, in the shadows where facts are twisted, and trust is broken. This is the new battlefield, where autocracies wage war without armies, using disinformation, economic pressure, and political manipulation to weaken their opponents. The fight is not on open ground but in the *Grayzone*—a space where the weapons are invisible, but the damage is all too real. And in this fight, democracies must decide whether to adapt or be dismantled.

CHAPTER FIVE

THE AI OF IT ALL

A rtificial Intelligence (AI) is no longer a distant dream—it is here, embedded in our daily lives, from voice assistants to automated stock trading to assisting in the creation of this book! The explosion of generative AI, machine learning, and large language models has reshaped industries at an unprecedented pace. But what's next? AI promises breakthroughs in medicine, energy efficiency, and creative arts, but also brings challenges—ethical dilemmas, regulatory hurdles, and a potential divide between those who wield AI's power and those left behind. This section will explore AI's trajectory, its disruptive potential, and the inevitable reckoning with its societal impact.

The pace of AI development is unlike anything humanity has witnessed before. Unlike past technological revolutions that unfolded over decades, AI is evolving at an exponential rate: each new iteration of models arriving faster, more powerful, and more refined than the last. By the time this book reaches your hands, the AI technology we have today may already feel outdated. The language models and image generators that currently push the boundaries of what machines can do will be eclipsed by even more capable systems, with better reasoning, multimodal abilities, and an uncanny grasp of human-like cognition. This acceleration is not just a matter of software improvements; it is driven by a self-reinforcing cycle where AI helps refine AI, making each new generation exponentially smarter and more efficient. The AI you interact with today—whether through chatbots, recommendation systems, or workplace automation—will likely seem primitive in just a few short years.

For years, the development of cutting-edge AI has been dominated by a handful of well-funded corporations and elite research institutions. Training the most advanced language models required staggering financial investments—hundreds of millions of dollars for computing power, specialized hardware, and vast amounts of data. This effectively locked out smaller players, leaving AI progress in the hands of a few tech giants, such as Meta, Microsoft, and the newer OpenAI. However, this dynamic has already begun to shift.

The emergence of Chinese company DeepSeek's model has upended conventional assumptions about AI development. Unlike previous models, which relied on expensive, high-performance chips and closed-source architecture, DeepSeek was trained at a fraction of the cost—reportedly under $6 million—using less powerful hardware.[1] Even more disruptive, DeepSeek has been released as open source, allowing anyone with the technical knowledge to build upon it. This innovation follows the pattern described by futurist Ray Kurzweil's Law of Accelerating Returns, which states that technological progress is exponential—each breakthrough enabling even faster and cheaper advancements in the next generation. This dramatically lowers the barriers to entry, democratizing AI development and potentially shifting the balance of power away from the monopolistic stronghold of Silicon Valley. With AI now more accessible and cost-effective, the future belongs not just to those with deep pockets but to those with the ingenuity to harness its power. And this is only the beginning. History has shown us that the average cost of producing technology is downward sloping, meaning that it will only get cheaper to create these models, which will serve more niche purposes, and millions of different use cases, further driving innovation.

The trajectory of AI is accelerating so rapidly that even its creators struggle to predict where it will lead. Unlike past innovations, which followed a near linear path of development, AI evolves in ways that are difficult to anticipate. Today's breakthroughs—models that can generate human-like text, create photorealistic images, and even code entire programs—are already redefining industries. But what comes next? Will AI surpass human cognitive abilities in unforeseen ways? Will it become a tool that seamlessly integrates into everyday life, or will it outgrow human oversight altogether? The possibilities range from utopian to catastrophic. Some envision AI solving the world's most complex problems—curing diseases, designing new materials, and revolutionizing energy production. Others warn of risks: mass job displacement, sophisticated disinformation, or AI systems making decisions beyond human control. One of the most profound uncertainties lies in the potential development of Artificial General Intelligence (AGI)—a system capable of human-level reasoning, learning, and adaptation across multiple domains. Unlike today's AI, AGI would not just follow instructions but would improve itself, potentially leading to recursive self-improvement—an AI that rewrites its own code, enhancing its intelligence at an accelerating pace. This could result in an intelligence explosion, where AI advances beyond human comprehension, making autonomous decisions that could reshape economies, geopolitics, and even the fundamental nature of power. Whether this future brings unparalleled progress or existential challenges remains unknowable. What is certain, however, is that AI will not stand still. The rate of progress ensures that the world of tomorrow will be shaped by machines whose full potential we can only begin to imagine today.

CONSEQUENCES

HOW AI AFFECTS DISCOURSE

The digital age has already tested society's ability to separate truth from fiction, but AI is rapidly escalating the challenge. With generative models capable of producing hyper-realistic images, videos, and audio at scale, misinformation is evolving beyond misleading headlines and doctored images—it is becoming indistinguishable from reality itself. In a world where people struggle to discern fact from fabrication, AI-driven misinformation threatens to erode trust in institutions, destabilize political discourse, and blur the very nature of truth.

The rise of AI-driven misinformation builds upon an already fractured information ecosystem. In the previous chapter, we explored how social media has reshaped discourse within and between nations—eroding traditional gatekeepers, amplifying extreme voices, and fostering an environment where engagement often outweighs accuracy. AI is accelerating this shift. Where social media once made it easier to spread misinformation, AI now automates its creation. Fake news, once reliant on human effort, can now be generated at scale with little cost or oversight. Deepfakes and AI-generated articles are no longer just tools of political operatives or propaganda machines—they are available to anyone with a computer and an internet connection. This convergence of AI and social media creates a perfect storm: an environment where falsehoods spread faster than ever, seamlessly integrated into existing ideological divides and algorithmic echo chambers.

AI's role in misinformation is undeniably growing. According to a 2024 report from the University of Florida, AI-enabled fake news websites increased tenfold in 2023 alone.[2] Many of these sites operate with little or no human oversight, generating fabricated news stories on autopilot. AI-powered misinformation campaigns can flood social media with fabricated political scandals, health conspiracies, or financial hoaxes at an unprecedented scale. While tech companies and fact-checkers are developing AI-driven solutions to counteract these threats, the arms race between generative AI misinformation and detection tools is only just beginning.

This convergence of AI and social media creates a perfect storm: an environment where falsehoods spread faster than ever, seamlessly integrated into existing ideological divides and algorithmic echo chambers. The question is no longer whether AI will shape discourse, but whether societies will be able to adapt to its influence before trust in information is irreparably broken. A stark example of this played out in March 2023 when AI-generated images of US President Donald Trump being arrested flooded Twitter (now X). These images, created using the generative AI tool Midjourney v5, depicted a dramatic, photorealistic scene of Trump being dragged away by police officers. The creator of the images, Eliot Higgins, initially intended them as satire, but their rapid spread ignited widespread concern about AI's ability to fabricate highly convincing false narratives.[3] While many viewers recognized the images as fake, the viral incident underscored a key danger: as AI-generated content improves, distinguishing between real and synthetic media will become increasingly difficult. The Trump arrest images were just a glimpse of what is to come—future AI-generated misinformation could be more subtle, harder to detect, and potentially weaponized to manipulate public perception.

One of the most alarming developments in AI-driven deception is the rise of telephone voice scams, where AI-generated voice clones impersonate real people to exploit their loved ones. Scammers use publicly available audio—often from social media or recorded messages—to create near-perfect replicas of a person's voice. With just a few seconds of speech, AI can generate an urgent plea for help, convincing family members that their loved one has been kidnapped, arrested, or is in desperate need of financial assistance. Victims, caught off guard by the familiar voice, often send money before realizing they have been deceived. As this technology improves, distinguishing between a real distress call and an AI-generated hoax will become increasingly difficult, further eroding trust in personal communication.

Even with heightened awareness of deepfakes and AI-generated misinformation, recent events suggest that public resilience against these technologies remains uncertain. The 2024 Indian general election, widely considered the world's first AI-influenced election, demonstrated how political actors are already deploying AI-driven misinformation tactics. AI-generated voice clones were used to impersonate political leaders, creating false endorsements and misleading messages. Meanwhile, deepfake videos of deceased politicians endorsing candidates circulated widely on social media.[4] Despite these efforts, the predicted "deepfake election crisis" did not fully materialize—many of the AI-generated fakes were quickly debunked. However, the incident revealed an evolving landscape where generative AI is a permanent fixture of political warfare. While India managed to contain the worst fears of AI-driven electoral chaos, the next major election—whether in the US or elsewhere—may not be as fortunate.

In the age of AI and social media, "believing is seeing." Social media platforms, powered by engagement-driven algorithms, create echo chambers where users are constantly fed content that reinforces their existing beliefs. Rather than encountering a broad spectrum of perspectives, people are shown news, opinions, and even AI-generated media that align with their worldview. This selective exposure strengthens ideological divides and makes misinformation more persuasive—because when people already believe something to be true, they are more likely to accept fabricated evidence that confirms it. As AI-generated content blends seamlessly into these digital environments, the challenge is no longer just separating fact from fiction but recognizing how personal biases shape what people choose to see as "real."

A Harvard Kennedy School study argues that fears about AI-driven misinformation may be overstated. While generative AI enables mass production of misleading content, misinformation researchers suggest that demand, rather than supply, dictates its influence. The study notes that misinformation consumption is concentrated among a small, highly engaged group of users rather than the general public.[5] Furthermore, misinformation is often spread not because of AI's capabilities, but due to pre-existing biases and distrust in institutions. As a result, while AI accelerates misinformation's spread, the real battleground remains human psychology—people will believe what aligns with their worldview, AI or not.

As AI-generated content becomes more advanced and increasingly difficult to distinguish from reality, the small, highly engaged group of users who already consume and spread misinformation will become even more entrenched in their beliefs. When deepfakes, AI-generated news, and synthetic media align perfectly with their pre-existing worldviews, these individuals will not only reject opposing viewpoints but also distrust any attempt to correct misinformation. This will amplify political and ideological extremism on both ends of the spectrum, further dividing societies into isolated factions where each side exists in its own version of reality. The result will be a deeply fractured information landscape, where consensus on basic facts becomes nearly impossible and political polarization reaches dangerous new heights. In this world, AI is not just a tool for misinformation—it becomes a force that accelerates social fragmentation, making it harder for democracies to function, for institutions to maintain legitimacy, and for people to agree on even the most fundamental truths.

As AI continues to blur the lines between truth and fabrication, the way people process information—and whom they choose to trust—will become more unstable. The rise of AI-generated misinformation is not just a technological problem but a societal one, deepening political divides, undermining institutions, and reshaping how reality itself is perceived. The challenge ahead lies not only in detecting falsehoods but in maintaining a shared understanding of truth in an era where seeing is no longer believing.

For populists and authoritarian governments, AI is not just a tool—it is a gift. The ability to manufacture reality is a power that past dictators could only dream of. If "believing is seeing," then AI allows those in power to dictate what people believe by controlling what they see. Imagine a world where a government seeks to justify its nuclear weapons program. AI-generated images flood social media, depicting a beautiful, glowing sunset. The catch? The "sunset" is actually a nuclear explosion, but the public, having never seen one firsthand, embraces it as a symbol of national pride. Soon, state-controlled AI chatbots reinforce the narrative—telling citizens that nuclear strength is not just security but beauty, progress, and power. Before long, people do not just accept the bomb—they love it. They demand it.

This is not science fiction. It is a logical endpoint of AI-powered propaganda. With AI's ability to generate fake videos, alter historical records, and flood digital spaces with state-approved narratives, authoritarian regimes no longer need to suppress the truth—they can simply replace it. AI can rewrite history, erasing inconvenient facts and reshaping past events to serve the ruling power's agenda. A censored search engine will ensure that dissenting voices never surface. AI-driven social media bots will amplify state-approved messages while drowning out opposition. Reality itself will bend to serve those in power. As AI becomes more sophisticated, the question is no longer whether authoritarian regimes will use it—it is how long before the people they deceive willfully defend their own manipulation.

Yet misinformation is just one of many ways AI is transforming society. Beyond manipulating narratives, AI is also reshaping economies, politics, and even warfare. While some fear AI's ability to deceive, others worry about its potential to displace workers, shift global power dynamics, and redefine the very nature of conflict. The next question is clear: as AI infiltrates industries and geopolitical strategies, what happens to the people left in its wake?

HOW AI AFFECTS THE JOB MARKET

Every technological revolution has displaced workers, but AI's impact could be unprecedented. Jobs once thought safe—law, finance, and even medicine—are now vulnerable. Customer service is being automated, content creation is AI-driven, and software engineers may soon compete with code-generating bots. As AI reshapes employment, it will fuel the same economic anxieties that have driven populist movements worldwide. What will happen when millions of workers realize that their expertise is no longer needed? This section will examine how AI-driven automation will exacerbate social inequality and political instability.

The initial wave of AI-driven automation is transforming the workforce, particularly in roles involving routine tasks and customer interactions. Jobs such as data-entry clerks, telemarketers, and retail cashiers are increasingly susceptible to AI replacement. A notable example is the call-center industry, where AI-powered virtual agents are rapidly taking over tasks traditionally handled by human employees.

An illustrative personal experience highlights this shift: one of the authors of this book recently called to schedule a massage appointment at a very nice hotel. The representative over the phone had a bit of an accent but was very knowledgeable about scheduling, types of massages, and their respective benefits. It was only after a few minutes of conversation that it became evident that the "representative" was, in fact, an AI bot. Although it took this author a few minutes to figure out the representative was AI, distinguishing between human and AI interactions will only become more challenging in the future, until one day we might not even notice, or care about, the difference.

The implications for the global workforce are significant. Globally, the number of call-center employees is estimated to be around 17 million.[6]

With AI systems capable of handling customer inquiries more efficiently and at lower cost, a substantial portion of these jobs is at risk of displacement. For instance, Klarna, a Swedish payments company, implemented AI chatbots that effectively replaced the work of 700 employees, reducing average issue resolution time from 11 minutes to 2 minutes.[7] As AI continues to advance, the challenge will be to manage this transition in a way that mitigates economic disruption and addresses the social implications of widespread job displacement.

Throughout the early 20th century, telephone operators played a crucial role in connecting calls, serving as the human link in an era before automated switching systems. At its peak, the profession employed hundreds of thousands of workers, mostly women, who manually routed calls through vast switchboards. However, as direct-dialing technology advanced, these jobs began to disappear. By the mid-century, automated switchboards had largely replaced human operators, and jobs declined by 50–80% over the course of just a few decades.[8] The transition was swift and unavoidable—technology had outpaced the need for human labor, rendering once-secure jobs obsolete. While many of the younger women were able to pivot to other jobs, the most experienced operators were left behind.

This same pattern is now unfolding in the call-center industry, where AI-powered virtual agents are rapidly replacing human representatives. Just as the switchboard automation of the past eliminated the need for operators, today's AI-driven chatbots and voice assistants handle customer service requests faster and more efficiently than human workers. Millions of jobs in call centers worldwide are at risk of vanishing, as companies adopt AI to cut costs and increase response times.

Call centers are only the tip of the iceberg—AI-driven automation is poised to disrupt a wide range of industries far beyond customer service. In finance, AI-powered algorithms are increasingly handling tasks once performed by junior accountants and financial analysts, automating everything from data reconciliation to risk assessment. In the legal field, AI tools can now draft contracts, review case law, and even assist in legal research, reducing the need for entry-level lawyers. Meanwhile, manufacturing—already transformed by robotics—is entering a new phase where AI-powered machines can not only assemble products but also predict maintenance issues, optimize production lines, and manage logistics with minimal human oversight. Even creative fields, once thought immune to automation, are seeing disruption. AI-generated content is reshaping journalism, marketing, and entertainment, with machine learning models capable of writing articles, composing music, and generating high-quality visuals. As AI continues to evolve, entire job categories may shrink or disappear, raising urgent questions about how economies and workforces will adapt to this next wave of technological transformation.

The people who lose their jobs to AI will not accept it quietly. Mass layoffs and the erosion of once-stable career paths will not be seen as the inevitable march of progress but as a direct betrayal—by corporations prioritizing efficiency over people, by governments failing to protect their livelihoods, and by a system that seems rigged against them. When jobs disappear, they do not simply vanish into abstraction; they take with them financial security, personal identity, and social stability. A displaced accountant or call-center worker may not have the luxury of retraining for a new career, especially when AI is also encroaching on those fields. For many, automation will not feel like innovation, it will feel like theft.

This sense of loss and alienation will only fuel the rising tide of populism. History has shown that economic uncertainty breeds political unrest, and AI-driven job displacement is set to deepen existing societal fractures. As more people find themselves economically sidelined, they will look for someone to blame—corporate elites, tech billionaires, political leaders, or even the very institutions meant to protect them. Trust in governments and financial systems will erode, mirroring past periods of industrial upheaval where economic anxiety translated into political radicalism.

The narrative will write itself: "The system is failing you." Populist movements will seize on this anger, using AI-driven job loss as yet another example of a broken establishment that serves only the wealthy and powerful. If AI is allowed to reshape the workforce without safeguards, it will not just disrupt economies—it will destabilize societies.

The stakes extend far beyond economics—who controls the AI narrative will shape the future of democracy itself. If left unchecked, AI-driven job displacement could become a weapon for authoritarian regimes and illiberal movements, capitalizing on public resentment to dismantle democratic institutions. If people believe that AI exists solely to enrich the elite while leaving them behind, they will turn to leaders who promise to take back control—often through radical, anti-democratic means. This is why it is critical for democracies to lead the charge in both AI development and regulation. The power to shape AI's role in society must rest with governments that are accountable to the people, not with corporations or authoritarian states that prioritize control over freedom. If democracies fail to set the rules, others will. The question is no longer just about who builds the most advanced AI—it is about who ensures that AI serves the many, not just the few.

THE GLOBAL AI ARMS RACE

AI is more than just an economic force—it is a geopolitical weapon. The race to develop the most advanced AI models is a modern-day arms race, with nations vying for dominance. The US and China lead this technological battlefield, investing billions in AI research with military and strategic implications. But this competition extends beyond governments—corporate giants like OpenAI, DeepMind, and Microsoft are battling for supremacy in AI research. The consequences of AI leadership will shape global politics, influence economic power, and potentially determine which nation dictates the ethical boundaries of AI.

China has long recognized that AI is not just a technological breakthrough—it is a pillar of global power. While the US currently leads in AI research, China is rapidly closing the gap, investing billions into AI development with a clear goal: technological self-sufficiency and global leadership. Beijing's strategy is aggressive, with government-backed firms pushing forward in AI research, often with state support and fewer regulatory restrictions than their Western counterparts. According to the Organisation for Economic Co-operation and Development (OECD), China has already surpassed the EU in AI research spending and is projected to exceed US total AI investment in the near future. This comes after President Trump announced a $500 billion investment in AI infrastructure in the US, to both create jobs and ensure that US-created AI products are more innovative and powerful than their Chinese counterparts. Unlike the private sector driven approach in the West, China's AI strategy is deeply intertwined with state priorities, focusing on both commercial applications and military advancements. From AI-powered surveillance systems to autonomous warfare technologies, China views AI as a tool for both economic dominance and geopolitical leverage. The question is no longer whether China will compete with the US in AI—it is how soon it will achieve parity or even superiority.

And it seems as though China may have already reached the point of parity in terms of Large Language Model (LLM) technology. The emergence of DeepSeek illustrates this view. What makes DeepSeek particularly significant is its cost efficiency and open-source model. Unlike US-based AI models that require extensive computing power and expensive proprietary datasets, allegedly DeepSeek was developed at a fraction of the cost, making advanced AI far more accessible. However, the exact cost of development of DeepSeek is disputed, with SemiAnalysis, a semiconductor research firm, estimating total expenditures to be over $500 million.[9] By releasing its architecture as open source, DeepSeek is enabling developers worldwide, particularly in China, to refine and deploy AI technologies without relying on American tech giants. This shift poses a direct challenge to Western AI leadership. If China can produce powerful AI models at a lower cost and distribute them widely, it could reshape global AI dynamics, reducing reliance on US technology and expanding China's digital influence. As AI becomes more integrated into search engines, chatbots, and research tools, the ability to manipulate information at scale could become one of the most powerful instruments of digital authoritarianism.

While the future of LLMs is unknown, what is clear is that China has some strategic benefits from DeepSeek's emergence: disrupting the US leadership of AI productivity and calling into question the efficacy of US sanctions intended to keep China in second place with technology.[10] With AI becoming an essential component of economic growth, access to information, military strategy, and global influence, the battle between DeepSeek and OpenAI is more than just a competition between tech firms—it is a geopolitical contest that could determine the future of digital power.

AI IN WARFARE

The race for AI dominance is not just about economic power or technological prestige—it is about military supremacy. The nation that leads in AI development will not only control the future of industry and information but will also dictate the future of warfare. Just as past technological revolutions—nuclear weapons, precision-guided missiles, and cyber warfare—reshaped global military strategy, AI is now emerging as the next defining force in combat. Autonomous drones, real-time battlefield analytics, AI-powered cyberattacks, and predictive warfare models are no longer theoretical—they are being deployed in conflicts right now.

The AI of It All

The US and China both recognize this reality, pouring billions into AI-driven military research, each vying to ensure that they, rather than their adversaries, dictate the rules of engagement in the wars of the future. Whoever controls AI will not just control industry, discourse, and labor; they will control the battlefield itself.

The war in Ukraine has become a testing ground for AI-driven military technology, particularly in the use of autonomous drones: airborne, sea, and unmanned aerial vehicles (UAVs). Unlike past conflicts, where drone strikes were primarily controlled by human operators, Ukraine has deployed AI-powered drones that can identify, track, and engage targets with minimal human intervention. These drones use machine learning algorithms to adjust flight paths, detect enemy positions, and strike targets with unprecedented precision. Every day in Ukraine, the sky is filled with countless drones, with as many as 1000 visible within a 24-hour period. Ukrainian interceptor drones have successfully neutralized over 850 Russian drones, yet certain areas of the battlefield remain so heavily monitored by aerial surveillance that soldiers refuse to enter, knowing they are constantly being watched and targeted.[11] The result is a battlefield where AI, rather than human soldiers, is making split-second decisions about life and death. The effectiveness of these systems has reshaped military strategy, with Ukraine using AI-guided drones to target Russian supply lines, armored vehicles, and even high-ranking military personnel. This is warfare at machine speed, where software updates can mean the difference between success and failure, and where human oversight is gradually being reduced in favor of automation.

The integration of AI into military operations in Ukraine is not just a regional development—it is a glimpse into the future of global conflict. As more nations adopt AI-powered drones and autonomous weapons, the nature of warfare will shift away from human-led combat to machine-driven engagements. More importantly, who will have the final authority to strike a target—the human operator or the AI-powered drone itself? Democracies may lean toward maintaining human oversight, prioritizing ethical considerations and accountability. Other regimes, however, may choose a more "efficient" approach, allowing AI to make life-and-death decisions with minimal human intervention. In warfare, these seemingly small differences in decision-making speed may determine the course of a conflict, shaping its escalation, its casualties, and, ultimately, its outcome. Additionally, these technologies raise ethical and legal challenges: if an AI-guided drone mistakenly targets civilians, who bears responsibility—the programmer, the military, or the machine itself? The lessons from Ukraine's AI-driven warfare will not only shape future conflicts but will also force policymakers to confront the urgent need for international regulations on autonomous weapons before AI-driven conflicts become the norm.

As AI-driven warfare advances, fewer human soldiers will be needed on the front lines. Autonomous drones can conduct airstrikes, AI-powered surveillance can track enemy movements in real time, and robotic ground units can engage in combat without risking human lives. This shift will reduce the traditional costs of war—not just financially, but politically. In past conflicts, the prospect of losing thousands of soldiers served as a powerful deterrent against military engagement. But if war can be fought with minimal human casualties, will governments be more willing to wage it?

This dynamic will introduce a dangerous new era of warfare. If AI can analyze threats, select targets, and even execute attacks with limited human oversight, the threshold for military action could become dangerously low. Leaders may be more inclined to initiate conflicts or escalate tensions, knowing that their own citizens will not bear the immediate cost. Moreover, AI-driven cyber warfare and autonomous provocations could be used to pressure adversaries, manipulate international relations, or even trigger conflict without clear accountability. With AI in control, war may no longer be fought solely by human decision-makers—it may become an ongoing, automated process, where nations continuously test each other's defenses with fewer political or ethical restraints.

AI-driven warfare is no longer confined to nation-states. As AI technology has become more accessible and dramatically cheaper, it is no longer just powerful governments deploying autonomous drones, surveillance tools, and cyber warfare systems. Criminal organizations, cartels, and extremist groups are now gaining access to AI-powered weapons, shifting the nature of conflict from state-controlled battlefields to decentralized, unpredictable violence. Drug cartels can use AI-enhanced drones to smuggle contraband, track law-enforcement movements, or even conduct targeted assassinations. Organized crime networks can deploy AI-powered cyberattacks to disrupt financial systems, manipulate markets, or evade surveillance. This democratization of AI-driven warfare means that violence is no longer limited to traditional conflicts between countries—it is spreading into the hands of non-state actors who can wield AI to challenge governments and security forces on an entirely new level. The future of warfare will be defined not just by global superpowers—it will be shaped by whoever can afford and effectively deploy AI for their own strategic gain.

The integration of AI into warfare is already a reality. From AI-guided drones in Ukraine to autonomous targeting systems in Gaza, the world is witnessing a transformation in military strategy that is unfolding in real time. The race for AI superiority is not just about economic dominance or technological advancement; it is about securing military power in a world where battles will increasingly be fought by machines, guided by algorithms, and decided in milliseconds. The consequences of this shift will extend far beyond the battlefield. AI-driven conflicts raise profound ethical, legal, and strategic questions that the world has barely begun to address.

Yet warfare is only one dimension of AI's impact on society. Beyond military applications, AI is already reshaping economies, disrupting labor markets, and redefining global power structures. As we look ahead, the critical question remains: What does the future of AI hold for us?

CONSEQUENCES

THE DOUBLE-EDGED SWORD OF AI

Artificial intelligence is both a marvel and a menace. It has the power to cure diseases, improve efficiencies, and revolutionize human creativity. But it also will threaten job markets, disrupt political stability, and alter the very fabric of truth. How societies adapt to AI's rise will determine whether it becomes a force for progress or a catalyst for crisis. Will AI serve humanity's best interests, or will it spiral beyond our control? The answer to that question will define the coming decades.

AI is not just a technological breakthrough; it is a force that will define the balance of power in the ongoing *Grayzone* war. Unlike conventional conflicts, this war will not be fought with tanks or missiles, but with narratives, influence, economic pressure, and technological dominance. Democracies must grapple with AI's potential to disrupt labor markets, fuel populism, and erode institutional trust, while autocracies weaponize AI for surveillance, censorship, and military control.

The stakes could not be higher. Whoever controls AI will control the future. If democracies fail to lead in AI innovation and governance, they risk ceding not just technological dominance but ideological control to regimes that will use AI to strengthen authoritarian rule. In this new era, AI is both a tool and a battleground, shaping the world's next great power struggle. The challenge ahead is clear: will AI be harnessed to protect freedom, or will it be used to accelerate control? The answer will determine whether democracy prevails in the digital age.

AI has undoubtedly changed the world as we know it, and its impact will only grow in ways we cannot yet fully comprehend. It is already reshaping economies, warfare, and political power structures—but more subtly, it is also changing how we perceive reality itself. In fact, AI has already influenced you and your perception and biases as a reader. If something felt slightly off about this chapter, you may have been onto something—because it was generated with the assistance of an AI LLM. Some of you may have suspected as much, but for those who did not, consider this: this will not be the last time AI alters your perception of what is human and what is not.

This is precisely the challenge AI presents to the modern world. As its presence becomes more seamless, more integrated, and more indistinguishable from human creativity and decision-making, the question of control will become more urgent than ever. AI is not just a tool; it is a battleground—one that will define the future of governance, warfare, truth, and power. Whether it strengthens democracy or accelerates autocracy will depend on who shapes its development, who sets its limits, and who ensures it serves humanity rather than dominates it. The world is now at an inflection point. The future of AI is unwritten, but one thing is certain: its influence is no longer a distant possibility—it is already here.

CHAPTER SIX

LIVING IN THE GRAYZONE

The ongoing struggle between China, Russia, and the world's democracies is often labeled a "new Cold War." However, this comparison misses the mark. The term "Cold War" implies a tense but static standoff, much like the 20th-century rivalry between the US and the Soviet Union, where mutual nuclear deterrence kept direct conflict at bay. Today's geopolitical landscape is far more volatile. This is not a cold war. Instead, it is a conflict unfolding in the *Grayzone*, a space where battles are fought without formal declarations of war but with very real consequences.

In the *Grayzone*, the war is already "hot." Russia's brutal invasion of Ukraine has shattered post–Cold War assumptions about security in Europe. Meanwhile, the looming threat of a Chinese military move on Taiwan raises the stakes in the Indo-Pacific. These events are not isolated; they signal a broader shift in global conflict dynamics. Unlike the Cold War, where nuclear equilibrium—*Gleichgewicht*—froze direct hostilities, today's *Grayzone* conflicts must be actively managed and, ultimately, won.

This struggle is not theoretical. It is unfolding now, with shifting alliances, economic warfare, cyberattacks, and proxy battles shaping the future of global power.[1]

GRAYZONE DEFINED

Military strategy guides define *Grayzone warfare* as conflict that stops just short of open war; opponents using every hostile measure short of war itself. *Grayzone* warfare refers to the use of non-traditional means. This new battlefield is murky, filled with covert tactics such as cyberattacks, propaganda, and subversion, to achieve strategic goals while avoiding direct military confrontation. *Grayzone* warfare seeks to exploit the ambiguity and uncertainty inherent in these situations to achieve advantage over opponents. This situation is not black and white—it is many shades of gray.

This is unlike the Cold War of the previous century. The equilibrium of a cold war depends upon high-impact, low-probability events such as mutual nuclear destruction. *Grayzone* war entails the opposite, high-probability, relatively low-impact events, such as cutting a pipeline or cables or invading a remote island. Escalation is almost inevitable in a *Grayzone* war and, apart from weapon development and deployment, almost impossible in a cold war.

Should Russia begin to lose in Ukraine, China will likely step in, even if it harms its own economy. Why? China would see Russia's fall as a threat to authoritarian strength worldwide. A decisive victory for democracy in Ukraine would be too great a blow. Conversely, if Russia wins, Europe's stability would crumble, and America's global leadership would face serious challenges. Of course, US hegemony may have morphed into isolationism before that. If so, that would be a negative feedback loop that would weaken the ability of democracy to defend itself.

Living in the Grayzone

PICKING SIDES

This leads us to the formation of global alliances. As mentioned earlier, on one side is the *Axis of Autocracies*, led by China with Russia supporting as a secondary power, alongside North Korea and Iran. Opposing them is the *Alliance of Democracies*, headed by the US. The authoritarian bloc stands on one side, the democratic coalition on the other.

Then there are the *N-Factor states*, which we will define as countries that do not align with either major alliance. Often mislabeled as the Global South (where most countries exist geographically) or grouped under BRICS (which is an official organization of nations created by Brazil, Russia, India, China, and South Africa to challenge Western dominance), these nations operate independently but remain under the influence of larger powers. They represent well over half of the world's population, with countries like India, Brazil, Indonesia, Turkey, the Gulf States, South Africa, and Saudi Arabia among them. With an estimated 70% of the world's population living outside of the "West" and China, these nations cannot be ignored.[2] Many of these nations are attempting

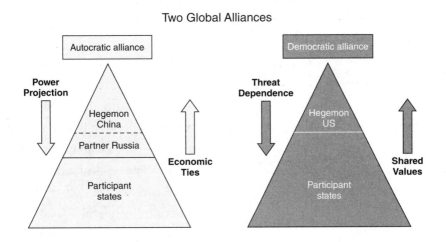

to avoid picking sides, such as Saudi Arabia, which maintains close relations with the US, China, and Russia simultaneously.[3] This indecision helps keep the balance of power between these two influential alliances, but with such a large number of *N-Factor* states in the middle, eventually the scale will tip to one side. While some nations may be pressured, most need to be persuaded to join one side. For instance, despite receiving cheap oil from Russia, India is unlikely to fully align with China's so-called Global South bloc.

Many *N-Factor* states are drawn to this Chinese-led alliance for several reasons: their colonial pasts (especially since many democratic nations in Europe were former imperial powers), past Soviet support for their independence movements, admiration for China's organized and economically successful system, and disappointment with capitalism's failures, such as poor COVID-19 responses, climate inaction, and rising inequality. These factors, along with poor internal management, make it difficult for the democratic alliance to convince these nations to join its distant cause. In fact, according to a study done at the Bennett Institute for Public Policy at Cambridge University, "Across a vast span of countries stretching from continental Eurasia to the north and west of Africa... societies have moved closer to China and Russia over the course of the last decade. As a result, China and Russia are now narrowly ahead of the US in their popularity among developing countries."[4]

N-Factor states likely lack enough shared interests to form a unified group—BRICS nations are proof of this. What this means is each unaligned nation will have to decide for themselves which path they will take. Although a single nation aligning with autocracy will not kill democracy, it could still cause disruption through direct partnerships with major powers like China or Russia. For example, Saudi Arabia's oil deal with China strengthens the use of China's currency (RMB) over the US dollar (USD), includes arms-for-oil exchanges, raises China's influence in the Middle East, and weakens US control in the region and over global oil prices.

This is in part because China and Saudi Arabia have discussed doing oil deals without the use of the USD as the exchange currency, and the countries' central banks have even agreed to a direct currency swap.[5]

Bilateral alliances often form around energy and commodity trade, but sometimes they are built on shared beliefs, like viewing autocracy as more efficient than democracy. Emerging governments may align with autocratic powers to maintain tighter control over their inhabitants, viewing centralized authority as a more effective way to suppress dissent and manage economic challenges. This alignment offers them a model of stability and control that democracy may not guarantee. Why gamble with power in a free election when you can rig the results and sleep soundly at night? The *Alliance of Democracies* can only counter the appeal of autocracy by setting a strong example and providing better opportunities to *N-Factor* states. However, it is important to recognize that the current rule-based global system is at risk. If *N-Factor* states reject it, it could collapse into a club for wealthy nations rather than a true global order, turning shared global values into narrow, partisan interests.

Alliances have a powerful impact on economies and markets, not just politics. Countries within alliances trade goods, share technology, hold international reserves, and engage in cultural exchanges. However, ongoing *Grayzone* conflicts threaten to disrupt these connections, creating serious risks for global economies and financial markets.

China's economic incentives like the Belt and Road Initiative and the Global Development Initiative, and the Asian Infrastructure Investment Bank has gained widespread participation, reinforcing China's narrative of providing an alternative to Western-led financial institutions. The Belt and Road Initiative specifically involves agreements with over 150 countries concerning Chinese-financed infrastructure development.[6] While participation in these projects does not necessarily mean that countries fully align with China's worldview, the large number of states involved enhances China's global legitimacy and strengthens its position as a key driver of economic growth in developing regions, to expand its influence. Though presented as aid, these projects are also strategic tools that increase China's global reach.

Additionally, China capitalizes on lingering resentment toward former colonial powers and promotes its autocratic system, which appeals to governments that already lean toward authoritarian rule or have weak democratic institutions. China has formalized its challenge to the liberal world order through strategic policies that prioritize the right to basic living standards over individual freedoms. In this model, the state holds ultimate authority, deciding how those living standards will be met, placing government control above the rule of law and personal rights. *N-Factor* states are increasingly drawn to China's model as its rapid rise to global dominance showcases how centralized control can drive economic growth and political stability.

The key difference between the *Alliance of Democracies* and China's alliance network is their foundation: the *Alliance of Democracies* is built on defending shared values, while China's alliances focus on expanding its influence, weakening democracies, and spreading its own model of governance. Imagine these alliances as circles of influence with solid triangles

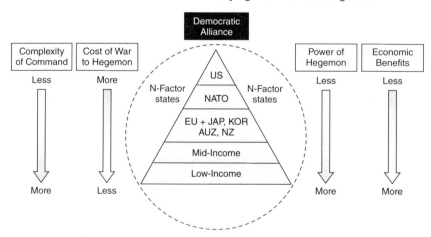

inside, representing firm alliances. The scattered dots around them symbolize *N-Factor* states, leaning toward one side or the other without officially joining.

The economics of the pyramid structure of an alliance means that as the pyramid widens to include more states, the power of the alliance increases, and the cost of war falls for the hegemonic nation that dominates the alliance. For example, if NATO were to be fully activated at the time of writing, the US would account for less than half the human assets and military hardware on the ground.

At the time of writing, the US-led alliance supporting Ukraine has wiped out much of Russia's military capabilities and likely crippled its ability to grow economically—achieved at a cost of approximately $175 billion in aid since 2022, about 20% of the US annual defense budget.[7] Still, the economic impact of alliances extends far beyond this. Countries within alliances typically trade more with one another, and studies show that alliance members hold 30% more of each other's foreign currency reserves than trade alone would suggest.[8] However, expanding alliances come with challenges. As the pyramid grows wider and taller, decision-making slows, enforcement weakens, and more effort is needed to keep the group united, requiring extra work to win back hesitant members.

OUTCOMES OF THE MULTI-POLAR WORLD

The rise of the *Alliance of Democracies* and *the Axis of Autocracies* makes two outcomes certain: the collapse of globalization and the return of active, interventionist governments.

Globalization is collapsing under the weight of its own failures, despite some successes. It created an open, rules-based system that allowed China to lift millions out of poverty through labor arbitrage—where companies outsourced manufacturing to China to take advantage of its cheap labor and lax regulations. This fueled China's rapid industrial growth and economic rise. However, globalization also widened global inequality, hollowed out manufacturing industries in wealthier countries, and let nations that ignored international rules expand their economic and military influence. It promoted the flawed belief that minimal government regulation and free markets would benefit everyone, a narrative that has proven only partially true. The idea that economic growth benefits everyone has proven misleading, as wealth has disproportionately flowed to the top while many workers and poorer nations have been left behind.

This imbalance also exposes the limits of the Law of Comparative Advantage, which as discussed above, assumes that nations can specialize in what they do best and trade freely to mutual benefit. However, labor is not interchangeable, unlike goods or capital, creating a mismatch in globalization's promises. Workers in wealthier countries often cannot compete with lower-cost labor abroad, while workers in poorer nations lack the protections or opportunities to fully benefit from global trade. This imbalance erodes the theoretical efficiency of comparative advantage, leaving many behind in an increasingly interconnected world.

In addition to deglobalization, widespread acceptance of government intervention will likely occur. While the level of involvement may vary across countries, governments will have a leading role in every key decision and policy area. Now, people expect their government to step in and take positive action, both in managing the economy and addressing social issues.

Beyond that, the *Grayzone* conflict is pushing nations to invest more heavily in defense. Japan, for example, is dramatically shifting its military strategy by doubling its defense budget to about $300 billion over 5 years, placing it among the top global defense spenders.[9] Historically, Japan relied on samurai swords, that is until Commodore Perry's arrival forced a rapid modernization, transforming the country into a major world power. While this did not turn out well the first time, Japan seems poised for another significant shift in its defense posture.

Achievement of Japan's defense ambitions will be challenging. The nation's demography means there is a shortage of young people. And many of those young people will not view a military career as attractive. This demographic challenge is significant because a smaller, less-willing youth population will limit Japan's ability to expand and modernize its military forces effectively. Similarly, aging populations across Europe pose similar threats to national security, reducing the pool of potential recruits and weakening long-term defense readiness.

These policy shifts—the collapse of globalization and return of activist, interventionist governments—are important and well-intentioned, but they will be difficult to accomplish without the *Alliance of Democracies* significantly cutting economic ties with China—and, to a lesser extent, Russia. In addition, any such separation will come with serious economic costs. Reducing global connections will lead to less cultural exchange and understanding, raising the risk of conflict. It will also cause fragmented trade, slower economic growth, and higher inflation. Geopolitical tensions usually drive inflation higher because they disrupt supply chains more than they reduce demand. For example, if you drop your phone in the sewer and need a replacement, but chip suppliers are under sanctions and production slows, you are out of luck. Demand will remain the same, pushing phone prices up as suppliers scramble to find scarce components, even through illegal means, causing chip prices to rise as well.

Globalization made production cheaper by creating deep, flexible supply chains that could easily adjust to demand. China's massive workforce entering global markets fueled the Great Moderation, a period of low inflation and falling interest rates. This gave people the sense of growing wealth, allowing them to buy more for less and borrow cheaply to afford things beyond their means. "Friend-shoring" and "on-shoring" will replace the efficiency of globalization with a focus on security, shifting from "just in time" to "just in case" supply chains. However, this added security will bring economic costs, such as lower productivity, higher inflation, and more market instability.

McKinsey reports that the share of global companies shifting to regional supply chains jumped from 25% in April 2021 to 44% by April 2022.[10] The European Central Bank warns that large-scale friend-shoring could shrink global trade by 12–19% and cut global GDP by up to 7%, depending on labor-market flexibility. Inflation could rise between 0.9% and 4.8% annually.[11] These forecasts assume a smooth transition, like Apple moving production from China to India, but real-world geopolitical tensions could make the impact much worse, especially in the short term.

While these negative outcomes are not guaranteed, one factor could make the situation even more severe. The costs of militarizing economies are not factored into friend-shoring estimates. Shifting to a war-focused economy raises inflation because defense spending increases wages and consumption, but it does not produce enough consumer goods to meet the rising demand created by those higher incomes.[12]

That said, we are less convinced that the increased military expenditure zaps innovation and productivity. Ukraine's war effort illustrates this point—rapid advancements in unmanned vehicles and drone technology have driven innovation beyond military use, benefiting other industries as well.

CURRENCY WARFARE

No part of the global economy is more vulnerable to *Grayzone* conflict than monetary and fiscal policy. This new kind of conflict is forcing a shift in how both are managed. Christine Lagarde, in a speech at the Council on Foreign Relations, explained that central banks must now focus on controlling inflation despite supply-chain disruptions, due to more inelastic supply chains than in prior decades.[13] Fiscal policy, she noted, should focus on removing economic bottlenecks rather than shielding everyone from the hardships of economic change. Programs like Europe's NextGenerationEU and "Fit for 55" green plan, along with the US Chips Act and Inflation

Reduction Act, help in this effort, whereas broad financial bailouts during energy crises will be less effective. These initiatives aim to boost economic resilience, drive green energy transitions, and strengthen domestic industries to reduce reliance on foreign supply chains.

International reserves are now a key battleground in the *Grayzone* conflict. China and several emerging markets are actively working to challenge the US dollar's role as the world's primary reserve currency. However, many policymakers and investors remain overly confident that this shift is unlikely to occur.

What is a global reserve currency? To hold this status, a country must have four main things:

1. The country must have a large and stable economy, along with strong trade and capital flows, to ensure its currency is widely available in global markets. Argentina would be an example of a country that fails this requirement, due to its relatively small economy and repeated economic crises marked by inflation, debt defaults, and currency devaluations.
2. The country must have a rule of law and solid institutions, to ensure that investors are protected by fair and predictable legal systems and financial agencies. Strong institutions and the rule of law ensure that contracts are honored, property rights are protected, and financial markets operate transparently. Without these safeguards, investors face high risks of asset seizures, capital controls, or arbitrary regulations, making it too risky to hold or trade that country's currency on a global scale. Russia is an example of a country that fails this requirement because of widespread corruption. Property rights and contracts are not consistently protected, which discourages foreign investors from holding Russian assets, as they cannot trust that their investments will be safe from government interference or sudden policy changes.

3. The country must have open and deep financial markets. This means there are large volumes of assets being traded, and a wide variety of financial products such as stocks, bonds, and derivates, that can be traded at a number of reputable banks or exchanges. Without these conditions, investors face higher risks and limited options, reducing a currency's role in global finance. As an example, one nation that does not meet this requirement is Turkey, which has been marked with high government intervention to control interest rates and inflation, as well as limited market depth in terms of investment options.
4. The country must have a currency that is easily convertible with plenty of safe government bonds for foreign investors to securely reinvest their funds. An easily convertible currency allows countries and businesses to quickly exchange it for other currencies, facilitating international trade and investment. Safe government bonds give investors a secure, low-risk place to store wealth, which keeps currency assets stable in times of economic crises or market volatility. A country like Egypt does not meet this requirement because the Egyptian pound is not freely convertible on international markets and, with frequent devaluations, Egyptian bonds are extremely risky.

These requirements perfectly describe the USD. It applies less to the Euro because there is a limited supply of safe EU bonds. The RMB does not fit these requirements. While the Chinese economy has reached that critical mass, the country's lack of openness and the RMB's lack of convertibility are holding it back. That is why the USD holds about 60% of global foreign exchange reserves at the time of writing.[14] Even if the USD were challenged, it would be nearly impossible to shift that massive share into much smaller currencies that make up only about 30% of global reserves—or just 10% if the euro is excluded.

However, this logic does not hold up well in the context of *Grayzone* conflict. These traits that define a global reserve currency are more a reflection of the USD's dominance than strict requirements. A challenger may not need to meet all these standards to compete in the future. China's RMB stands out as the most likely rival. Although it is not widely used internationally now, China's massive economy gives the RMB the potential to increase its global influence—and Beijing is actively working to make that happen. Through the aforementioned Belt and Road Initiative, the Cross-Border Interbank Payment System (CIPS) as an alternative to SWIFT, and currency swap agreements, China has made the RMB more appealing to other nations. However, China will not fully open its financial markets or capital accounts like the US or the EU. It faces a conflict between two goals: keeping the Chinese Communist Party firmly in control of the economy while simultaneously trying to expand its influence on the global stage.

Still, China can expand the global use of its currency. The RMB's role as a reserve currency has grown alongside China's expanding trade, even without fully open markets. A major factor in this growth is China's 39 bilateral swap agreements with other central banks, which help provide liquidity and legal support.[15] These agreements act as a substitute for the requirement of "full currency convertibility," making the RMB more usable internationally by providing both liquidity and legal legitimacy.

Some evidence backs this trend. The Society for Worldwide Interbank Financial Telecommunication (SWIFT) is a global messaging network that over 11,000 financial institutions use to securely exchange information about financial transactions. SWIFT data shows the RMB's share in global payments jumped to a record 4.47% by the June of 2024, up from 2.77% the previous year.[16] Additionally, settlements in China's currency for cross-border commodity trade have doubled every year since 2020, reaching 20% of China's total trade in 2023. However, the RMB's growth has mostly stalled since then. Its share of global currency reserves has not grown significantly recently. In fact, the RMB's share of global foreign exchange reserves has slightly declined to around 2.5% over the past 2 years.

The problem became clear when Russia invaded Ukraine. About $300 billion of Russia's foreign currency reserves held in Western countries, including the SWIFT system, were frozen. This move was widely criticized as the "weaponization" of international reserves.

It was not unreasonable to think that countries like China and those in the Global South would shift their reserves into other currencies and assets to avoid the risk of their funds being frozen and weaponized, as happened to Russia. However, this did not occur. Why not? There are three main reasons why countries did not shift away from the USD.

The first reason is size and dominance. As stated previously, the USD makes up nearly 60% of global trade and reserves. There is no other currency large or stable enough to replace it. The USD is deeply embedded in the global financial system, making it the standard for trade, investment, and reserve holdings.

The second reason is that the majority of global trade runs through the USD. Large currency trades often pass through the USD. For example, selling South African rand for Argentine pesos requires converting to USD first because those markets lack liquidity. This exposes trades to US sanctions, which apply worldwide to any transaction involving the US financial system.

The third reason is fear of China. *N-Factor* states, such as those in the Global South, worry that China could also freeze or control their assets, just like the US did to Russia. India, for example, has a history of border tensions with China and is unlikely to trust its reserves to China's central bank.

Alliances play a critical role in shaping global currency dynamics, especially concerning de-dollarization. Countries aligned with dominant powers, particularly the US, are more likely to stockpile the USD as a financial safeguard. This is not just theoretical; the data supports it. The International Trade Commission (ITC) defines "safe" USD assets as the money that foreign governments invest in US financial products. This includes US Treasury bonds, debt from government-backed agencies, and short-term loans to US banks. Over 50% of all foreign-held safe US assets are controlled by nations bound to the US through formal mutual defense treaties.[17] When nations engaged in broader military cooperation agreements with the US are included, this figure jumps to an impressive 75%.[18] This pattern underscores how security alliances extend beyond defense, embedding economic dependence on the USD. For instance, as highlighted in *Autocracy Inc.* by Anne Applebaum, authoritarian regimes often navigate these alliances cautiously, balancing economic benefits with political risks.[19] Simultaneously, China's ambitious Belt and Road Initiative reflects a strategic attempt to counter the US-centric financial order by fostering tighter economic ties with developing countries and promoting the RMB in cross-border trade.

Let us explore potential scenarios to understand how global reserves might shift, keeping in mind that the USD currently makes up around 60% of global foreign exchange reserves, while the euro holds about 20%.

Typically, there is a stable relationship between trade levels and currency reserves. If there was a 2% drop in trade between country A and country B, this would result in a 1% reduction in country B's currency held in country A's reserves. This ratio, however, is not fixed. Geopolitical events—such as economic sanctions, military conflicts, or shifts in alliances—can significantly impact how attractive a currency appears, causing this relationship to either strengthen or weaken. For now, the standard 0.5× ratio will be applied in these scenarios, though it will be increased to 1× in the final scenario to reflect the potential for greater sensitivity in times of heightened geopolitical tension.

Earlier in this book, we defined the *Alliance of Democracies* to include NATO members, the EU, neutral European states, Japan, South Korea, Australia, New Zealand, and ASEAN. If every country outside this alliance began invoicing all of their international trade conducted with countries beyond this group in Chinese RMB, the global share of USD reserves would decrease by only approximately 6%. Even if China further reduced its USD holdings by 10%, and Hong Kong pegged its currency to the RMB, the decrease in the US dollar's share of global reserves would change only from 6% to 10%. This highlights the entrenched position of the USD in global reserves, showing that even significant shifts toward alternative currencies like the RMB would not drastically alter the global financial balance.

Currently, as stated earlier, the USD makes up about 60% of global reserves. Let us factor in a stronger reserve-to-trade elasticity of 1%, influenced by geopolitical choices. Now, if we assume China reduces its USD holdings by 20% instead of 10%, the dollar's share of global reserves would fall decisively below 50%. Despite this decline, the USD would still hold its place as the world's largest reserve currency, though its dominance would be notably weakened.

While these assumptions are simplified and the scenarios might appear extreme, they highlight a critical point: in the event of escalating *Grayzone* conflicts—such as a potential war over Taiwan or direct Chinese intervention supporting Russia's war in Ukraine—even the most drastic reserve currency scenarios remain plausible. Although such shifts would likely unfold gradually, the possibility of significant geopolitical disruptions reshaping global financial dynamics cannot be dismissed. China has clear motivation to act against the USD's dominance, driven by the fear that its USD assets could be frozen, much like the sanctions imposed on Russia. Undermining the power of the USD would directly support China's objectives in *Grayzone* warfare, weakening the financial leverage of the US and advancing China's strategic goals.

However, it is important to note that if this occurred countries within the democratic alliance would likely increase their holdings of USD reserves and continue trading in USD—potentially rising at least 30% above historical levels. Additionally, citizens in these nations, along with a significant portion of wealthy individuals in the Global South, would still view the USD as a secure and stable asset. This would counteract any geopolitically driven attempts by China and the rest of the *Axis of Autocracies* to diminish its global dominance.

THE TRICKLE-DOWN EFFECTS OF *GRAYZONE* WARFARE

Grayzone conflicts can persist for extended periods, but eventually, one side must prevail, or both will face the devastation of full-scale war. In Ukraine, for example, there is a war of attrition. Escalating costs and the need for faster technological innovation result in both sides spending time and resources on a conflict that currently has no end in sight. Eventually, one side must give way and call for peace, otherwise they will be decimated both financially and militarily. Confrontations like this are marked by continuous escalation. Consider the aggressive actions that have occurred as the war has continued:

1. Severing undersea cables.
2. Assassination attempt on a CEO of a Western defense firm.
3. Efforts to place explosives on cargo planes destined for the US.
4. Attempts to contaminate urban water supplies.

This growing list of hostile acts signals an alarming trend toward greater conflict. Direct military action between the *Alliance of Democracies* and the *Axis of Autocracies* appears increasingly unavoidable. For instance, sustained provocations against Taiwan cannot continue indefinitely without eventually triggering direct military engagement.

The *Axis of Autocracies* is evolving from a loose and temporary coalition into a unified force driven by a shared ideology: the dismantling of democracy and the restructuring of the global order. This alliance is developing the capability to wage war across multiple theaters—simultaneously targeting the Asia-Pacific, the Middle East, and Europe—while enhancing the cooperation of its armed forces. As these nations expand their nuclear capabilities, the US's single-theater war doctrine for nuclear conflict, outlined in the Department of Defense's Strategic Guidance, has become outdated and ineffective. To confront this growing threat, the US must adapt to multi-theater warfare and its allies must share this responsibility. Failure to do so would allow the *Axis*, once it achieves superiority across regions, to strategically choose when and how to overpower the *Alliance* through war or the threat of war. This reality exposes the danger of isolationist policies like "America First," which could be one of the most shortsighted strategies ever proposed. In this context, unilateral action would be the costliest path, especially considering that 40% of US international trade and investments is tied to Europe—an economic relationship that could be jeopardized.

What will happen as a result of increasing *Grayzone* tensions is both unknown and unknowable. However, if the world continues down this path, most nations with major economies will most likely experience significant militarization over the next decade. Countries like Japan, Taiwan, and South Korea, historically reliant on US security guarantees, could shift from having no nuclear warheads to developing significant stockpiles. Additionally, governments will have to become larger and more interventionist, yet economic productivity and growth will remain sluggish while inflation stays elevated. This pattern will be further intensified by aging populations, which will place additional strain on economic performance and policy effectiveness.

As a result, central banks will likely be forced to adjust their targets to accommodate persistently higher inflation. Supply chains are expected to become more rigid and less adaptable, leading to sharper and more volatile economic and inflation cycles. In other words, productivity will suffer. This evolving environment will require a fundamental reassessment of how fiscal and monetary policies are designed and implemented.

Traditional drivers of growth in emerging markets will largely disappear as wealthier nations and China shift their focus inward, emphasizing service-based economies. Most emerging markets lack the economic scale needed to substitute export-driven growth with domestic consumption, leaving them potentially vulnerable in this changing global landscape.

Any decline in the USD's dominance caused by the efforts of the *Axis of Autocracies* to undermine it will likely be counteracted by greater reliance on the USD among *Alliance of Democracies* members. Additionally, many citizens and several nations within the Global South, motivated by both security and self-interest, will continue to favor the USD as a trusted financial asset. In short, the USD is here to stay.

However, the biggest factor is that a decline in cultural exchange could weaken our ability to empathize with and understand individuals from opposing blocs. This cultural isolation leads to intellectual impoverishment, making it harder to grasp differing perspectives. On a practical level, it can result in flawed intelligence and poor decision-making.

The outlook in this evolving era of *Grayzone* warfare remains deeply uncertain. The sweeping economic, political, and military shifts underway are reshaping global dynamics in ways that are difficult to fully predict. Nations are fortifying alliances, economies are turning inward, and traditional systems of global trade and finance are under strain. While some outcomes, like increased militarization, economic intervention, and fragmented global markets seem inevitable, the long-term consequences of these changes remain unclear. Will these pressures lead to greater resilience and cooperation among democratic nations, or will escalating tensions push the world closer to open conflict? The erosion of cultural exchanges and rising geopolitical distrust will only deepen this uncertainty, negatively affecting the ability of leaders to make informed decisions. As the *Grayzone* conflict intensifies, the path forward is uncertain leaving the global community to navigate an unpredictable and volatile future.

CHAPTER SEVEN

THE NOT SO MIGHTY GREENBACK

The previous chapter explored the complex dynamics of *Grayzone* warfare and its surprising impact on the USD as the world's dominant reserve currency. Despite mounting efforts by the *Axis of Autocracies*—nations like China, Russia, and others that challenge Western democratic norms—the USD remains firmly entrenched at the core of global finance. These regimes engage in subtle economic and political hostilities, from cyberattacks to strategic resource control, aiming to weaken the influence of democratic nations. Yet, ironically, these very tactics may be inadvertently bolstering the demand for the greenback. In times of geopolitical tension, global investors and governments instinctively seek safe havens for their wealth, and no currency offers the same combination of liquidity, stability, and trust as the USD.

This paradox underscores a critical point: while adversaries work to undermine the US's financial dominance, their aggression often triggers a flight to safety that strengthens it. However, external threats may not pose the greatest risk to the dollar's supremacy. The US could very well sabotage its own currency without any help from its rivals. Mounting national debt, persistent budget deficits, and political gridlock threaten to erode global confidence in the greenback—issues that receive close scrutiny in the pages that follow.

A NATION IN DEBT

At the time of writing, the US's sovereign debt exceeds 100% of its Gross Domestic Product (GDP), but this figure that understates the full extent of the problem. This is because it reflects only the net debt. The International Monetary Fund (IMF) reported that the gross sovereign US debt-to-GDP ratio reached 123% in 2023. Additionally, the US federal budget deficit currently stands at 6% of GDP, highlighting the growing imbalance between government spending and revenue.

According to the US Congressional Budget Office (CBO), if current policies remain unchanged, the nation's net sovereign debt is projected to rise to 118% of GDP and could soar to 195% by 2053. Historically, other nations have faced more severe sovereign debt crises with much lower debt-to-GDP ratios and budget deficits. It would take a shift in sentiment—such as bond market investors refusing to purchase or actively shorting US debt—for the US's financial stability to unravel completely.

Neither of the major political parties in the US has a clear strategy for addressing this dangerous financial trajectory. Meanwhile, the general public remains largely oblivious to the growing crisis. In fact, a Gallup poll from March 2024 showed that only 51% of participants responded that they worry "a great deal about Federal spending and the budget deficit," while 22% responded that they worry "only a little or not at all."[1] This issue was notably absent from discussions during the most recent election campaign, highlighting how unprepared the nation is for the challenges ahead. These circumstances create an ideal environment for financial disaster. The pressing question is not whether it will happen, but when. The fatal arithmetic of this looming financial crisis is relatively straightforward to understand.

The US consistently operates with a "current account" deficit, meaning it imports more goods and services than it exports. This imbalance effectively mirrors a national savings deficit, where the country spends more than it earns. The US does not save enough to cover both its investments in the real economy and its growing budget deficit. This shortfall amounts to roughly 3% of the nation's total income.

The savings deficit has two additional characteristics. To fully understand this concept, it is essential to define the relationship between GDP and national income. GDP measures the total value of all goods and services produced within a country, while national income represents the total earnings received by individuals and businesses from that production, including wages, profits, rents, and taxes (minus subsidies). These two figures must be equal because every dollar of production generates income for someone—whether it is paid to workers, business owners, or the government. This balance ensures that what the economy produces directly translates into income distributed throughout the economy, forming the foundation of national financial health.

A savings deficit reflects the gap between what the US economy produces and what it spends on consumption and investment—commonly referred to as aggregate demand. For simplicity, it is easier to think of this as overall spending, since most people relate more naturally to the idea of spending money than to the term "demand." The savings deficit also represents the gap between the income the US generates, national income, and the amount it spends.

At its core, the current account tracks how much the US borrows to finance the amount of spending that exceeds what it produces or earns. Since 2000, the US has consistently run a current-account deficit ranging from 3% to 6% annually. Over the past 25 years, this pattern means the country has spent twice as much as it has produced, covering the gap entirely through borrowing—and it has yet to repay any of this debt. As of mid 2025, the US foreign debt stands above 90% of its GDP, closely aligning with this estimate.

If the average country operated this way, its foreign debt would quickly reach 90% to 100% of its GDP. To simplify, consider this scenario: to sustain a current-account deficit of 3% of GDP, the country also runs a budget deficit of 6% of GDP. Half of that deficit is financed through national savings, while the remaining half is borrowed from foreign lenders. This accounts for the foreign debt, but the domestic debt is another issue—it would have expanded by an additional 75% of GDP.

If that does not signal financial collapse, it is hard to imagine what would. Countries must learn to live within their means, echoing the straightforward economic wisdom of former UK Prime Minister Margaret Thatcher. In her 1976 speech at the Conservative Party Conference she said, "We have first to put our finances in order. We must live within our means. The Government must do so. And we must do so as a country. We can't go on like this… We are spending more than we earn. The gap has to be bridged. It can only be bridged at present by borrowing from overseas. But it cannot be bridged that way for ever. And at any moment, if we forfeit the confidence of those who lend to us, that bridge can collapse. It is crumbling now. The only way to safety is to stop borrowing and stop borrowing soon; and, moreover, to show that we can and will repay our debts in a strong currency and on time."[2]

While this is a nice sentiment, the simple strategy of living within one's means will not work in the case of the US. This is because holding the world's reserve currency shields the US from immediate financial consequences.

Unlike other nations, the US can continue borrowing and spending beyond its means without triggering a crisis. That is until confidence in the USD erodes, and the situation suddenly turns critical.

A NEGATIVE FEEDBACK LOOP

A reserve currency functions based on several key factors, as discussed in the previous chapter. To reiterate, the four requirements are:

1. Critical mass in terms of its economy, trade, and capital flows, which includes an adequate supply of its currency to international markets.
2. The rule of law and robust institutions.
3. Deep and open capital markets.
4. A convertible currency with adequate supply of risk-free sovereign bonds to permit foreign holders of the currency to reinvest it safely in liquid assets.

The USD meets all these qualifications for being a global reserve currency. However, these very strengths carry hidden risks that could ultimately lead to its downfall. To understand why these strengths can become weaknesses, it is essential to first understand how a reserve currency like the USD operates to reveal underlying risks within the system.

As discussed above, the US consistently imports more goods and services than it exports. To cover these purchases, it must exchange USD for foreign currencies, leaving those USD with international suppliers. While some of these USD return to the US through payments for American exports, the trade imbalance ensures that a significant amount of US currency remains in foreign hands.

The USD held by foreign countries are often reinvested into US-based assets. Typically, these funds pass through foreign central banks, where they are converted into foreign exchange reserves. This happens because foreign sellers need local currency to cover expenses like wages and raw materials—depending on where those materials come from and how they are priced. As a result, these USD become liabilities for the US and assets for foreign central banks. This cycle is how the US effectively borrows from abroad to finance its savings shortfall.

During times of geopolitical tension, such as today, countries holding USD as international reserves might hesitate to continue doing so. This reluctance could stem from fears that their assets might be frozen—similar to what happened to Russia amid its conflict with the US—or from ideological opposition to the US-led global order, prompting them to avoid holding American assets altogether. A foreign central bank could choose to sell its USD to another country and instead hold that nation's currency as a reserve. However, this action would not reduce the overall presence of UAS in the global system. Regardless of who holds them, these USD remain a liability for the US and are ultimately invested back into US assets.

The global demand for the USD as a reserve currency continues to rise alongside the steady growth of international trade. The US economy functions like the fuel tank of a massive global engine—constantly supplying the USD needed to keep international commerce running smoothly. The US must pour more fuel into the tank each year by running larger and larger deficits, to keep the engine of international trade from sputtering out.

This system might seem sustainable, but there is a major problem: the US economy is steadily shrinking in proportion to global GDP. Statista data shows that the US share of global GDP, when adjusted for purchasing power, was 15.5% in 2024, a 0.5% drop from 2020, and this is projected to fall below 15% by 2027.[3] As developing countries expand and industrialize, this global economic growth is outpacing that of the US. Ironically, these emerging economies narrow the gap with the US by building strong manufacturing industries that export inexpensive goods to American markets, fueling international trade and accelerating their own growth.

The math behind this system is unsustainable. To meet the growing global demand for USD in international trade, the US must continually increase the supply of USD each year. However, every additional dollar supplied adds to the country's foreign debt. This debt is rising faster than the US economy itself, which limits the nation's ability to repay it. Since international trade must expand more rapidly than US economic growth to allow emerging markets to raise their living standards, the US is caught in a cycle where its debt grows faster than its capacity to manage it.

Eventually, the swelling burden of US debt compared to its GDP will collapse—much like an overloaded bridge strained by weight it can no longer support. Each additional dollar of debt adds more pressure, and without a matching increase in economic output to reinforce the structure, the bridge weakens. At some point, the strain becomes too great, and the entire system risks buckling under its own weight.

LOSS OF CONFIDENCE

The moment of financial reckoning could arrive in one of two ways. Domestic bond investors in the US might lose confidence and sound the alarm, or foreign investors could turn against US debt, triggering a crisis from abroad.

This is not just a problem that might occur; it already has. In the mid-1990s, Russia faced significant fiscal challenges, leading the government to rely heavily on short-term, ruble-denominated zero-coupon bonds, known as GKOs, to finance its budget deficits. Initially introduced in 1993, these zero-coupon bonds became a primary tool for domestic borrowing.

As the government continued to issue GKOs to cover its spending, the debt burden grew substantially. To attract investors, Russia offered increasingly higher yields, which, by 1998, had reached unsustainable levels. This strategy resembled a financial pyramid scheme, as new debt issuances were used to pay off maturing obligations.[4]

The situation deteriorated further when both domestic and foreign investors began to lose confidence in Russia's ability to service its debt. By July 1998, the government struggled to roll over its treasury bills maturing before the end of the year. This loss of investor confidence led to a sharp decline in demand for GKOs, effectively cutting off the government's primary funding source.[5]

Facing mounting pressure, the Russian government took drastic measures on August 17, 1998. It devalued the ruble, defaulted on its domestic debt, and declared a 90-day moratorium on the repayment of certain foreign debts. This default included the restructuring of GKOs and OFZs (longer-term federal loan bonds), transforming them into new securities with extended maturities.[6]

The default had a cascading effect on the Russian economy. The ruble's value plummeted, inflation soared, and the banking sector faced severe disruption, with many banks closing. The government's inability to meet its obligations eroded both domestic and international confidence, leading to a prolonged period of economic instability.

This episode underscores the dangers of excessive reliance on short-term debt instruments to finance budget deficits. When investor confidence wanes, the sudden withdrawal of funding can trigger a financial crisis. It is daunting to consider how much more severe a crisis like this could be if it involved a currency as widely used and deeply embedded in global reserves as the USD.

This presents a question: is it possible to create a global reserve currency that can sustain itself without leading to its own downfall?

SHIFTING COURSE

The answer is yes. A self-sustaining global reserve currency is possible—we once had one under the international gold standard. Back then, international reserves could expand as quickly as the global gold supply grew, creating a stable system. However, this stability came at a cost: only a few countries were able to develop and "emerge" economically. International trade was largely confined within colonial empires that used their own currencies, limiting broader economic growth. For many, daily life remained unchanged and isolated from global markets. Returning to such a system today would be nearly impossible.

A more modern proposal for a self-sustaining global reserve currency involves using the IMF's Special Drawing Rights (SDRs) to facilitate international trade. In theory, this could be an effective solution. However, significant challenges remain—such as determining how many SDRs should be issued and deciding who would control their distribution. It is difficult to imagine the US willingly ceding even partial authority over this system to China, a country that now holds influence over roughly 20% of United Nations institutions and would likely seek to politicize its role in this process.

History shows that major crises often drive meaningful reform, and the same will likely be true for addressing the US's growing debt and financial excesses. The tipping point could come when domestic bond investors lose confidence and turn against US sovereign debt. Alternatively, foreign investors might be the first to act, or both domestic and international markets could react simultaneously—either scenario would force the issue into a full-blown crisis.

At first glance, it might seem reasonable to assume that the impact would simply be a 3% decline in US GDP. This assumption is based on the idea that demand—through consumption and investment—exceeds the nation's output by that same percentage, mirroring the portion of the budget deficit not offset by domestic savings. However, this view is too simplistic and does not capture the true scale of the problem. The real issue lies in the existing stock of debt, not merely the rate at which it is growing. The core problem is not how quickly debt levels are rising but the overwhelming accumulation of liabilities that must be confronted and reduced.

An obvious but risky solution would be for the US to print more USD. As the issuer of the world's reserve currency, it could take advantage of what former President of France Giscard d'Estaing famously called its "exorbitant privilege." However, this approach would likely worsen the situation. Foreign investors might rapidly sell off USD, triggering a currency crisis on top of the existing sovereign debt problem. This would drive domestic inflation to dangerous levels, ultimately reducing the purchasing power of Americans and leaving them worse off.

For example, consider a scenario in which the US government needed to lower its debt level to 60% of GDP within the next decade to restore market confidence. This target mirrors the European Union's Excessive Deficit Procedure, which requires member states with debt exceeding 60% of GDP to implement corrective measures.

Achieving this goal would require the US to run a primary budget surplus of 4% of GDP annually. Currently, however, the US faces a primary budget deficit of 6% of GDP. A primary budget balance excludes interest payments on existing debt, focusing solely on government revenues and expenditures. While it would be nice to ignore the interest payments, they constitute about 2.4% of GDP annually, which adds to the issue. To meet this target, the government would need to reduce spending by 6% of GDP. While challenging, this is not entirely impossible—consider that federal spending on education alone accounts for about 6.4% of GDP. Eliminating that expense would technically close the gap, though such a drastic cut would have severe consequences.

To put this into perspective, other major areas of government spending include social security at 4.8% of GDP, Medicare and Medicaid at 5.4%, and defense spending at 3.0%, although substantial budget cuts in these areas would be politically and economically challenging.[7]

However, this is only part of the picture because economic multipliers come into play. In economics, a multiplier refers to how an external change can have a greater, amplified effect on the overall economy. For example, if a $100 billion project—regardless of its usefulness—were constructed using local labor, the economy would grow by more than $100 billion. This happens because the workers would spend their earnings on goods and services, further stimulating demand and increasing economic output.

Naturally, economic multipliers can also have negative effects. A clear example of this was the European Union's sovereign debt crisis when Greece's GDP per capita plummeted by 24% over a 4-year period. Addressing a debt crisis of this scale would require the US government to cut its non-defense spending by approximately 30% annually for the next decade to bring sovereign debt down to 60% of GDP.

Whether American democracy could withstand such severe spending cuts is uncertain. In a polarized society, it is doubtful that the public could unite to endure the hardship required. The blame for the crisis would largely fall on political parties that have ignored these growing risks, leaving them discredited in the eyes of the public. What political movements or leaders might rise to fill that void is unpredictable—and potentially more troubling than the current state of governance.

Regardless, the escalating national debt and the government's inability to address it pose the most significant internal threat to the stability of US democracy. However, the US is not alone in facing such risks. Other developed nations like France, Germany, Italy, and Spain also confront similar vulnerabilities. That is a discussion for another time.

The future of the USD—and by extension, the global economy—hinges on choices yet to be made. The weight of unchecked debt, political inaction, and growing global competition is not a distant threat but a looming reality. Whether the US can adapt, reform, and stabilize its financial foundation will determine more than just economic outcomes; it will shape its role in a rapidly evolving world order. If history teaches us anything, it is that no currency, no matter how dominant, holds its throne forever. What rises to replace it, or whether the USD can be fortified for the challenges ahead, remains uncertain. But one truth is clear: the clock is ticking, and the consequences of inaction will not wait.

CHAPTER EIGHT
IMMIGRATION

The US is often called a nation of immigrants, a testament to its history of welcoming people from across the globe. The US is unique in the world as the vast majority of citizens can trace their origins to another land, a legacy rooted in the earliest settlements like Plymouth and Jamestown, forged through the Revolutionary War, and expanded with the waves of immigrants who passed through Ellis Island. This blend of diverse cultures, skills, and ideas has been fundamental to US success as an economic and political powerhouse. Shouldn't the successes of the US be the "proof of the pudding" that immigration works? Instead, in recent years, immigration has become one of the most contentious issues, fueling debates across dinner tables, political platforms, and international summits.

For many populist movements, immigrants are an easy scapegoat. Populist rhetoric thrives on identifying enemies—groups that can be blamed for complex social or economic challenges. Immigrants often fit this narrative neatly, not because of any inherent truth but because their presence can be mischaracterized. Whether due to cultural differences or economic anxieties, immigrants are framed as threats to jobs, safety, or national identity. This framing persists despite overwhelming evidence that immigration is not only essential but also economically beneficial.

In developed economies, immigration is more than a cultural phenomenon; it is an economic lifeline. Populations in countries like the US, Germany, and Japan are aging rapidly. This can be seen by their change in age dependency ratio (the number of individuals aged 65 and older divided by those aged 15 to 64). In the US, this ratio grew from 0.126 in 1950 to 0.223 in 2018. In Japan, it rose from 0.09 in 1960 to 0.46 in 2018.[1] As birth rates decline and life expectancy increases, the number of retirees relying on social support grows, while the pool of working-age citizens shrinks. Working-age migrants can fill critical gaps in the labor force, ensuring a steady supply of workers in industries where labor shortages are most acute. Immigrants also contribute to government revenues through taxation, which is crucial for sustaining the social welfare systems that face rising costs due to aging populations.

Productivity and innovation per capita also decline as a population ages. Immigrants help bridge this gap. They contribute as workers, innovators, and consumers, ensuring that economies remain dynamic and able to sustain their populations. The Partnership for a New American Economy discovered in 2012 that three out of four patents issued to America's most prestigious universities with the top 10 highest patent output had one foreign-born inventor or more.[2] An IMF study conducted in 2020 showed evidence that immigrants in advanced economies boost both output and productivity in the short and medium term.[3] Although populists would like you to believe otherwise, there is minimal evidence to show that immigration leads to lower wages and fewer available jobs.[4] Many times, immigrants take the least desirable jobs, which existing citizens do not want. Without immigration, many nations risk stagnation or even contraction, a reality underscored by the IMF and numerous economic studies.

CHALLENGES

The presence of immigrants is often met with varying levels of tolerance by native populations, particularly when it comes to the integration of foreigners into their communities. Social cohesion and comfort levels can influence how willingly local populations accept new arrivals, shaping the dynamics of immigration policies and societal integration.

Economic capacity sets another boundary on immigration, particularly in terms of job availability. The demand for labor depends on the number of positions that need to be filled, while the supply is shaped by the willingness of both native citizens and immigrants to take those jobs. Striking a balance between the two is critical to ensuring that labor markets remain stable and inclusive. This is where things begin to get challenging.

Even with a sharp decline in global fertility rates—from an average of 3.5 children per woman in the 1980s to 2.3 today—world population is still projected to grow. Over the next 25 years, it is expected to increase from 8 billion to 9.7 billion by 2050, eventually reaching a peak of 10.4 billion by 2100.[5]

It is worth pausing here to reflect on the ideas of Thomas Malthus, who, in his 1798 work *An Essay on the Principle of Population*, argued that wages would naturally stabilize through grim means: death, not benevolence. According to Malthus, if wages exceeded the subsistence level, populations would grow rapidly, like rabbits, only to outstrip resources. Conversely, if wages fell below that level, starvation would ensue, reducing numbers. This bleak cycle, in his view, was inevitable and self-regulating. Either we would become too gluttonous, or too malnourished, and the size of the global population would level out again.

Malthus was ultimately proved wrong. High birth rates did not lead to wages falling below subsistence levels because diseases frequently claimed the lives of children before they could enter the workforce. Interestingly, the number of young people per family reaching working age in the

18th century, during Malthus's time, was similar to that of the mid-20th century. The key difference was the dramatic decline in birth rates by the 20th century, a shift largely attributed to improvements in public health, such as the introduction of sewer systems, antibiotics, vaccines, and better access to clean water, which significantly reduced mortality, specifically for infants, which in turn reduced the need to have more children.

BACK TO TODAY

In recent decades, medical advancements have significantly extended life expectancy in both poor and wealthy nations. As a result, even though fertility rates have steadily declined, the global population has surged, creating a labor supply that far outpaces the ability of economies to absorb it.

Naturally, this issue is not evenly distributed across the globe. In developed economies, medical progress has also led to increased longevity, resulting in a growing number of retirees. According to the World Health Organization, "global life expectancy has increased by more than 6 years between 2000 and 2019—from 66.8 years in 2000 to 73.1 years in 2019."[6] However, if we compare a country like Japan, with a life expectancy of 85.2, to Somalia, 56.5, you can see how this issue is only a problem in some countries.[7] This shift has lowered the ratio of active workers to dependents, creating a labor shortfall. To fill this gap and sustain the production of goods and services demanded by retirees, these economies increasingly rely on immigration.

This demographic shift has created another significant challenge: a fiscal one. In most developed countries, governments are responsible for funding retirees' consumption rather than their contributions to the workforce. Pension systems and healthcare expenditures for aging populations place immense strain on public finances. As retirees live longer due to advances in medical care, the costs of sustaining these benefits escalate, creating a growing gap between the resources available and the increasing demands of aging populations. This economic imbalance results in the urgent need for the solutions to problems such as immigration and for policy reforms to mitigate the fiscal burden.

In poorer nations, population growth far outpaces the creation of jobs, leading to widespread unemployment and underemployment. This economic disparity drives large waves of migration, as individuals and families seek better work opportunities and living conditions elsewhere. For instance, countries like Nigeria and Ethiopia in Africa face rapid population growth alongside limited economic opportunities, while nations in South America, such as Venezuela and Honduras, struggle with economic instability and unemployment, further exacerbating migratory pressures. Many migrants are drawn to wealthier countries, where they hope to escape poverty, access stable employment, and build a future for their children. In addition to economic challenges, wars and widespread violence in countries like South Sudan, the Democratic Republic of Congo, and El Salvador compel many to flee, as individuals seek refuge from conflict, persecution, and the dangers that make everyday life untenable. These migratory movements, while offering hope for individuals, also bring complex challenges for destination countries, including the need to balance labor-market demands, integration efforts, and social tensions.

In many ways, the advancements in medical science have outpaced the ability of global economies to adapt to their consequences. While these innovations have extended life expectancy and reduced mortality, they have also contributed to challenges such as overpopulation and labor-market imbalances.

Over the next 15 years, half of the anticipated 1 billion person increase in the global population will occur in Africa, with another 40% in poorer Asian nations. Unfortunately, many of these countries are ill-equipped to support their growing populations, lacking the economic infrastructure and resources needed to provide acceptable living standards for their citizens. According to *The Economist*, "On current trends, Africans will make up over 80% of the world's poor by 2030, up from 14% in 1990,"; this issue has been compared to climate change and nuclear war in terms of threats to our world.[8] This anticipated increase in wealth disparity highlights the urgent need for development strategies and international collaboration to address these challenges. For this rise in population to see an equal rise in productivity, there will need to be large-scale investment and improved governance; that is a lot easier said than done.

The challenges faced by these countries are further compounded by the effects of climate change, which reduces arable land, exacerbates food and water shortages, and increases the likelihood of state failure. These issues are intensified by the "brain-drain" phenomenon, where educated and skilled individuals from poorer nations migrate to developed economies in search of better opportunities, leaving their home countries with even less help and innovative thinking to address these escalating crises.

As a result, immigration can generally be categorized into two distinct types: large-scale movements of people fleeing failed states in search of basic safety and survival, and a smaller, more selective group of skilled refugees or qualified professionals seeking opportunities in developed economies.

GLOBAL REACTION

Regardless of whether a country is governed by democratic principles or autocratic rule, the approach to managing large-scale immigration often looks strikingly similar. This typically involves erecting physical or metaphorical barriers, such as fortified borders, strict offshore detention centers, and policies of forced repatriation to keep unwanted masses from entering.

This approach to immigration control cannot be solely attributed to figures like Donald Trump. European nations, such as Germany and France, are already implementing strict measures to curb immigration.

Germany has tightened its asylum laws, increased deportations, and negotiated agreements with third countries to manage migrant flows. France, meanwhile, has intensified border checks and established offshore processing centers to regulate entry. Immigration strategies transcend political systems; whether a government is democratic or autocratic, such measures reflect the current reality and are likely to persist.

Beyond the fortified borders of developed economies, the world faces escalating conflicts among failed states, including wars over scarce resources like water and food. Disease will emerge as an unchecked mechanism, disproportionately affecting vulnerable populations, while climate change will exacerbate the crisis. According to the BBC, rising sea levels threaten to engulf at least seven major cities located in low-lying areas, and agricultural devastation caused by extreme weather will further undermine food security. These interconnected disasters paint a grim picture of the challenges awaiting those outside the relative safety of wealthier nations.

Fortunately, mass and social media provide us with real-time coverage of these unfolding crises, ensuring that no disaster goes unnoticed. However, this constant exposure rarely leads to action. Instead, the barrage of images and stories often desensitizes us, fostering a sense of indifference. Over time, we become hardened and detached, viewing these tragedies with a pragmatism that borders on moral apathy. Pope Francis described the current state of humanity as having "fallen into a globalization of indifference."[9] He explained that the comfort and prosperity many of us experience have fostered selfishness and a lack of empathy for the daily suffering and pain endured by others worldwide. Social media has inured us to become spectators of tragedy, yet the constant stream of global disasters has numbed us, leading to inaction. This reality underscores why the potential turn toward isolationism among Western nations could have such harmful consequences.

The looming tragedy lies in the impracticality of freely moving labor across borders in a world where production factors rarely flow seamlessly between nations. This inherent imbalance highlights a fundamental flaw in globalization: it has often failed to deliver tangible benefits to workers, who are left disconnected from the opportunities promised by globalization.

IMMIGRATION'S BENEFITS

This reality does not validate the anti-immigration rhetoric often championed by populists, who frequently label immigrants as freeloaders or criminals. Such claims are unfounded and misleading.

Research indicates that immigrants are less likely to commit crimes than native-born citizens. A study by the National Bureau of Economic Research found that in 2020, immigrants were 60% less likely to be incarcerated than US-born individuals.[10] Similarly, a 2020 study focusing on Texas revealed that undocumented immigrants have substantially lower crime rates than native-born citizens across various felony offenses.[11] It is essential to manage immigration thoughtfully, ensuring that policies are driven by rational considerations rather than prejudiced or incorrect assumptions about those seeking refuge in wealthier nations.

Numerous research studies on the economic impact of immigration in the US reveal that the post-COVID immigration wave contributed an additional 0.1–0.3% to annual GDP growth. While this percentage may seem modest, the actual monetary value is substantial, amounting to approximately $500 billion annually.

In Europe, the IMF has reported that "the recent migration has helped accommodate strong labor demand, with around two-thirds of jobs created between 2019 and 2023 filled by non-EU citizens, while unemployment of EU citizens remained at historical lows. Ukrainian refugees also appear to have been absorbed into the labor market faster than previous waves of refugees in many countries. The stronger-than-expected net migration over 2020–23 into the euro area (of around 2 million workers) is estimated to push up potential output by around 0.5 percent by 2030—slightly less than half the euro area's annual potential GDP growth at that time—even if immigrants are assumed to be 20 percent less productive than natives. This highlights the important role immigration can play in attenuating the effects of Europe's challenging demographic outlook."[12]

Research on immigration in the UK indicates that, over their working lifetimes, immigrants contribute significantly more in taxes than they consume in public resources. This data challenges the stereotype of immigrants as "spongers," and seems particularly ironic in a nation that partially justified its departure from the EU based on curbing immigration.[13] In the US, data provides no evidence that immigrants exhibit higher levels of criminality compared to native-born citizens.

These findings effectively debunk the false narratives surrounding immigrants who have successfully settled in host countries. While the cited studies focus on individual nations, the broader data indicates that such stereotypes about immigration do not hold up to scrutiny.

Nonetheless many immigrants are turned away. What is the solution to their plight?

Right now, there is no definitive solution. It appears that maintaining democracy comes with the challenge of regulating immigration—both in terms of numbers and skill levels—to ensure it aligns with the needs of a thriving economy. Populists are quick to exploit fears that this balance might not be achieved.

This chapter concludes that democracy is as flawed as populism in its approach to immigration. Both systems often resort to ethically troubling policies when addressing the challenges posed by migration. While it is an uncomfortable truth, it remains a reality.

As we look ahead, the question of immigration forces us to confront not only our economic and political priorities but also the values that define us as societies. The challenge is not merely logistical or economic—it is profoundly human. The future will demand innovative solutions that go beyond building walls or crafting policies that serve only the immediate interests of a select few. It will require balancing pragmatism with empathy, ensuring that the forces driving migration—conflict, climate change, and inequality—are addressed at their roots. The way we navigate these complexities will shape not only the demographics of tomorrow but also the moral and social fabric of the world we leave behind. If we fail to rise above the simplistic narratives and divisive rhetoric, we risk perpetuating cycles of exclusion and suffering. But if we choose to engage with these issues thoughtfully and compassionately, there is a chance to create a future where borders do not define the limits of our humanity.

CHAPTER NINE

THE HEART OF THE MATTER

L et's go back in time. WWII called for immense sacrifices from the US and its allies. The US alone invested an estimated $4.1 trillion, with military spending peaking at nearly 40% of the nation's GDP in 1945.[1] These numbers reflect only the financial burden; the human cost was even more profound. Over 418,000 American soldiers gave their lives in the effort to defeat the *Axis* powers. Other nations endured similar, if not greater, losses—be it in lives, infrastructure, or resources. This collective commitment highlights the extraordinary measures taken to preserve freedom during one of history's darkest chapters.

In contrast, at the time of this writing, the US has provided $100 billion in aid to Ukraine, while European nations have contributed $150 billion. These amounts represent just 0.37% of the US GDP and 0.79% of the EU GDP, a fraction of their economic capacity.

In truth, these contributions are mere rounding errors, far from meaningful sacrifices. The aid has been limited, hesitant, and poorly planned, often disrupted by the US. Much of the provided material has been carefully chosen to avoid provoking Putin to escalate the conflict further. This aid often falls short not only in quantity but also in quality. Much of the military support is comprised of outdated weaponry, decommissioned vehicles, and surplus equipment that Western nations no longer find practical for their own forces. While these contributions have served as stopgaps, they have been far from adequate for Ukraine to achieve a decisive edge on the battlefield. Advanced technologies such as modern air defense systems and precision-guided weapons—critical for countering Russian aggression—have been provided sparingly, leaving Ukraine to make do with insufficient resources. In fact, for example of the missiles provided to Ukraine do not have enough range to reach to most important Russian targets. This patchwork approach to aid indicates a lack of commitment to Ukraine perpetuating a conflict that could otherwise be shortened with decisive and strategic support. Crucially, this support has never been sufficient to equip Ukraine to secure a decisive victory—and now, there is the growing possibility that it could cease entirely.

While most of us take pride in the support provided to Ukraine, we ought to feel shame. The assistance is paltry—just enough to ensure that Ukrainians continue to fight and die for a cause that ultimately serves our interests: the defense and survival of democracy.

SOLUTIONS

What is needed to address the ambitions of autocratic leaders like Putin? This conflict is a defining moment for the preservation of our way of life. The *Axis of Autocracies* reflects troubling parallels to the Fascist Axis of the 1930s, reminding us of the importance of vigilance and unity. By taking decisive steps today, we can avoid the far greater human and economic costs of future conflicts. The cost of a future war, both human and economic, will likely be far greater than that of World War II. This is not just a challenge—it is an opportunity to strengthen democratic alliances and secure a stable and prosperous future for generations to come.

Yet, in the US we continue to act as though we are not at war, avoiding the declaration of clear war aims. Such a denial makes it easier to retreat and ignore the looming threats. Russia, naturally, seeks to exploit this confusion, hoping we will become passive and disoriented. Such inaction would allow Putin to dismantle democracies one by one without firing a shot—just as he has already done in Georgia and nearly accomplished in Moldova and Romania.

The most straightforward path to victory against the *Axis of Autocracies* is to decisively and kinetically defeat its weakest link on the battlefield. Economically, Russia's power is limited; its economy is comparable to Italy's in size. Even in terms of purchasing power parity (PPP), Russia's GDP accounts for only 12% of the combined $60 trillion GDP of NATO member states.[2] These statistics should leave no doubt: the democracies hold the clear advantage. If we throw our full support behind Ukraine, this conflict will cease to linger, as it has for over 3 years at the time of writing this book.

The real question is how much of our GDP we, as democracies, are willing to dedicate to the fight against Russia. In a dictatorship like Russia, citizens have no say in such matters, allowing the regime to allocate 8–9% of its GDP to the conflict. We contribute very little by comparison. However, our economic strength means we do not need to match Russia's percentage—a mere additional 1–2% of GDP provided by NATO countries would generate 600 billion, surpassing Russia's military budget by five to six times. This increase would elevate the *Alliance of Democracies* total military spending to roughly 4% of GDP, a necessary target considering the simultaneous need to contain China.

Even if Russia is forced out of Ukraine, Russia will need to be contained. There is little doubt that Putin's grip on power will be shaken, but what comes next—whether a renewed authoritarian regime or a chance for reform—remains uncertain. Russia lacks any tradition of democratic governance. The nation may even be headed for an economic collapse, but rebuilding Russia is not our responsibility. Our focus should remain on rebuilding Ukraine, while Russia isolates itself behind a metaphorical high fence. Compromising with Russia would allow it to rebuild its military and return to threaten Europe—targeting countries like Poland, the Baltic States, Romania, and the Caucasus—within just a few years.

There are doubts about whether democracies have the resolve to rise to this challenge. Over time, complacency and internal divisions have eroded the vigilance needed to safeguard democratic values. However, history has shown that democracies, when faced with existential threats, are capable of remarkable resilience and unity. This moment provides an opportunity for renewal—both in strengthening democratic institutions and in proving that shared values can overcome even the most daunting adversities.

One possible, but highly unlikely, solution would be the introduction of military service across all democracies. Such a program could unite troops from various member nations of the *Alliance of Democracies*, fostering units that represent shared values rather than individual national identities. This approach would not only strengthen collective security but also reinforce the bonds of cooperation and mutual understanding among allied nations.

THE CREATION AND DISTRIBUTION OF WEALTH

The foundation of a thriving democracy lies in prioritizing two major things: the creation of wealth and a more equitable distribution of that wealth within economic policy. For democracy to endure, citizens must feel a sense of ownership and investment in its success. Once this foundation is established, other critical components—such as inclusive education and social programs—become both achievable and sustainable.

Data from Freedom House highlights a strong positive correlation between democratic values and higher living standards, including metrics like wealth per capita. Freedom House's *Freedom in the World* report assesses political rights and civil liberties across nations, assigning scores that reflect the state of democracy in each country. While the report primarily focuses on political freedoms, it often highlights the broader benefits of democratic governance, including higher living standards. For instance, countries rated as "Free" typically exhibit higher levels of wealth per capita compared to those classified as "Partly Free" or "Not Free." This correlation underscores the positive relationship between democratic values and economic well-being.

Moreover, the report provides detailed analyses of individual countries, often noting how declines in democratic practices can lead to economic downturns, while strengthening democratic institutions can foster economic growth.[3] These insights further support the connection between robust democratic values and improved living standards.

No society can maintain civility and stability without prioritizing wealth creation. Research indicates that societies emphasizing wealth creation tend to experience greater political stability and social cohesion. For instance, the IMF highlights that economic growth is essential for poverty reduction and improved distributional outcomes, which are crucial for maintaining a stable and just society.[4] Additionally, author Francesco Duina notes that civility promotes productive economic activity and wealth, which are central to political stability.[5] These findings suggest that prioritizing wealth creation not only enhances economic prosperity but also reinforces the social and political frameworks that uphold civility and stability. Wealth creation serves as the most effective mechanism for allocating productive capital, fostering the development of stable middle classes, and ensuring the economic security of retirees.

Wealth represents a stock of assets, distinct from GDP, which functions as a flow. GDP, however, serves as the "river" that feeds into and sustains the "lake" that is wealth. To ensure this flow contributes effectively, it must be guided by meritocracy while avoiding the pitfalls of extreme wealth inequality.

Different countries have achieved equitable wealth distribution through various approaches, with Finland and Sweden serving as notable examples. In Finland, policies such as progressive taxation and comprehensive social welfare systems have been instrumental in promoting economic equality. Similarly, Sweden has implemented robust public services and labor-market policies that support income redistribution. These strategies have not only fostered social cohesion but also contributed to dynamic economies. The effectiveness of these approaches is reflected in the high levels of happiness reported by their citizens. According to the 2024 World Happiness Report, Finland ranks as the world's happiest country with a score of 7.74, while Sweden holds the fourth position with a score of 7.40.[6] This correlation suggests that equitable wealth distribution and comprehensive social policies play a significant role in enhancing overall well-being.

The Gini coefficient is a widely used measure of income and wealth inequality, providing insight into how economic resources are distributed within a society or across the globe. It ranges from 0 to 1, where 0 represents perfect equality (everyone has the same income or wealth) and 1 indicates extreme inequality (one individual possesses all the income or wealth). Over the past few decades, globalization has lifted millions out of poverty, yet the gap between the world's richest and poorest remains stark, with some estimates placing the global Gini coefficient above 0.6, signaling a deeply uneven distribution of wealth. In the context of global wealth distribution, the Gini coefficient highlights significant disparities between and within nations.

For instance, according to the World Bank, South Africa has one of the highest Gini coefficients globally, indicating substantial income inequality.

Conversely, countries like Norway and Slovakia have lower Gini coefficients, reflecting more equitable income distribution.[7] These variations underscore the diverse economic landscapes worldwide and the challenges in addressing income inequality.

While Finland and Sweden are often celebrated for their equitable wealth distribution, these policies are not without challenges. In Sweden, high taxes intended to fund generous social programs have led some wealthy individuals and businesses to leave the country, seeking lower-tax jurisdictions. This trend has sparked concerns about a potential "brain drain," as some of the most innovative and entrepreneurial individuals relocate abroad, weakening the country's long-term economic dynamism. Furthermore, such redistributive systems can exacerbate the "free-rider" problem, where individuals benefit from extensive public services without contributing proportionately to their funding. Critics argue that this imbalance risks undermining the sustainability of Sweden's welfare model, as the burden on remaining taxpayers grows while public resources are stretched to accommodate those contributing less. These issues highlight the complexities and trade-offs of achieving equitable wealth distribution.

The role of government is pivotal in fostering a fair and cohesive society. Citizens are generally willing to pay taxes when they perceive tangible value in return, such as quality public services and infrastructure. Without this trust, resistance to taxation grows, undermining the government's ability to perform its vital redistributive functions—functions essential for rebuilding and sustaining a thriving civic society.

Ultimately, different cultures and nations will choose varying policy approaches to achieve inclusive wealth distribution. However, failing to prioritize this goal puts democracy at risk. Rising polarization can fracture societies, creating vulnerabilities that authoritarian regimes—the so-called *Axis of Autocracies*—are quick to exploit. In summary, democracy's greatest threat lies in the dangerous convergence of internal populism and external pressures from the *Axis of Autocracies*.

CHAPTER TEN

THE LAST CHAPTER

The cover of this book captures our concern about the future of democracy in a world where "reality" is not so "real," as it is now influenced and shaped by an onslaught of social media and artificial intelligence. This final chapter is not just a conclusion—it is a call to action.

Democracy, once thought to be self-sustaining, is proving to be far more fragile than once thought. In the past, truth was debated, but at least there was a shared foundation of facts. Today, the digital age has shattered that foundation. Truth is now a fluid concept, molded and reinforced by social media algorithms that amplify outrage and artificial intelligence is further distorting public perception. If democracy depends on an informed citizenry, what happens when people can no longer agree on what is real? This is the challenge we face—not just an erosion of democratic norms, but an erosion of reality itself.

CONSEQUENCES

THE ISSUES RESTATED

The attack on the US Capitol on January 6, 2021, was more than a violent outburst—it was a stress test for American democracy. In the wake of the insurrection, national leaders and legislators invoked the words of Benjamin Franklin from an era long ago when he was asked, "What kind of government have you delivered us?" His response, "A republic, if you can keep it." That phrase, first spoken in 1787 as the US Constitution was finalized, was a warning, and it remains one now. The endurance of democracy is never a given; it depends on the collective will of the people to uphold it. History reminds us that republics do not collapse overnight. They erode when institutions weaken, when civic trust disintegrates, and when leaders place power above principle. If January 6 revealed anything, it was how fragile democratic norms have become—and how urgently they must be reinforced.

Today, a more pressing question emerges: Are we still a democracy, or are we drifting toward autocracy? Warning signs exist. In their 2018 book *How Democracies Die*, political scientists Steven Levitsky and Daniel Ziblatt dissect the slow erosion of democratic norms and institutions. In their final chapter, Saving Democracy, they make a sobering point—there is no constitutional safeguard or cultural immunity that prevents democratic backsliding. A republic does not survive on laws alone; it survives on the willingness of its people and leaders to uphold democratic principles. History is clear: the US has faced moments of extreme political crisis before, from the Civil War to the struggle for civil rights. In fact, one could argue that true democracy in America began with the passage of the Voting Rights Act in 1965. That moment was a step forward—but it was not the end of the fight. The same forces that once sought to suppress democracy have evolved, and today, they are using new tools to challenge it.

Since *How Democracies Die* was published in 2018, two powerful forces have dramatically reshaped the political landscape—social media and artificial intelligence. These technologies have not just altered communication; they have fundamentally changed how people perceive reality itself. In the past, "seeing was believing." Today, that phrase has been turned on its head. Now, "believing is seeing." Individuals no longer seek out facts; instead, they gravitate toward information that reinforces what they already believe. Social media platforms, driven by algorithms optimized for engagement rather than truth, fuel this phenomenon by trapping users in echo chambers of confirmation bias. Meanwhile, artificial intelligence is accelerating the problem. Deepfake videos, AI-generated misinformation, and bot-driven propaganda campaigns blur the line between truth and fiction like never before. In a democracy, where an informed public is essential, the consequences of this shift cannot be overstated. If people can be convinced to doubt objective reality itself, how can they be expected to make informed political decisions?

The transformation between 2018 and 2025 is staggering—perception has overtaken reality. We no longer live in a world where people disagree on policy; we live in a world where they disagree on basic facts. This shift has had profound consequences. In the US, Donald Trump has returned to the White House, winning a very large plurality but not a majority of votes. Yet what sets this moment apart from previous political battles is not just the outcome—it is the unprecedented role of these social media and AI in shaping public perception. These technologies have done more than influence opinions; they have redrawn the very fabric of political reality, creating a landscape where objective truth is optional, and belief is weaponized.

Levitsky and Ziblatt argue that American democracy has historically depended on two unwritten norms: mutual tolerance and institutional forbearance.[1] Mutual tolerance means recognizing political opponents as legitimate actors rather than existential threats. Institutional forbearance is the idea that those in power should exercise restraint rather than exploiting every legal advantage at their disposal. These principles have never been formally codified into law, yet they have served as the foundation of stable governance. Without them, democratic institutions still exist on paper but lose their effectiveness in practice.

Put another way, democracy is not just a set of laws and institutions; it is a system of habits, understandings, and shared commitments. Laws provide the framework, but the unwritten agreements between political leaders and citizens are what make it function. When these norms erode, democracy does not collapse overnight, but it becomes increasingly dysfunctional. Rules can be manipulated, elections can be undermined, and power can be concentrated in ways that remain technically legal but fundamentally undemocratic.

At its core, democracy depends on two values: freedom and equality. These ideals do not sustain themselves. They require constant reinforcement, political leaders willing to abide by democratic principles, and citizens who actively defend them. Without vigilance, these values can fade into hollow rhetoric, leaving behind institutions that look democratic but no longer serve their intended purpose.

The greatest threat to American democracy is not a foreign adversary or a sudden authoritarian takeover—it is the deepening of an internal division. Partisan divides have widened along paths like race, religion, and economic inequality. These divisions are not new, but in the past, shared democratic values acted as a bridge across them. Today, that bridge is collapsing. Social media has not just amplified these divisions; it has accelerated and hardened them. Algorithms ensure that the most polarizing content spreads the fastest. Instead of fostering debate, online platforms have turned political identity into a battlefield, where opposing views are not just different but irreconcilable.

The consequences of this polarization are profound. When citizens see their political rivals as enemies rather than fellow participants in democracy, compromise becomes impossible. Governing turns into a zero-sum game. Institutions that were designed to encourage debate and consensus instead become tools for obstruction and domination. This cycle feeds on itself, driving people further into their ideological corners and making constructive dialogue nearly impossible.

Levitsky and Ziblatt highlight a striking observation from their colleague, Harvard Professor of Political Philosophy, Danielle Allen: "The simple fact of the matter is that the world has never built a multiethnic democracy in which no particular ethnic group is in the majority and where the political equality, social equality, and economies that empower them all have been achieved."[2] This is not just an academic insight—it is the fundamental challenge for the US and all democracies worldwide. As demographic shifts continue, US is navigating uncharted territory, attempting to build a truly inclusive democracy in a society without a single dominant ethnic majority. History offers no blueprint for success, only warnings about the dangers of failing to meet this challenge.

Importantly, this is not just the US's challenge—it is democracy's challenge. When ethnic diversity increases, economic inequality widens, wages stagnate, and partisan divisions deepen. These tensions have always existed, but today they are amplified by social media and artificial intelligence, which accelerate outrage and harden ideological divides. When people feel left behind economically, or see their cultural identity as under threat, resentment grows.

In a TED talk on the global state of democracy, Stanford Political Science Professor Larry Diamond outlines a troubling pattern followed by authoritarian populists around the world. Their strategy does not rely on military coups or outright declarations of dictatorship. Instead, they operate from within democratic systems, using legal and institutional tools to consolidate power while maintaining the appearance of legitimacy. First, populists frame the existing political establishment as irredeemably corrupt, casting all opponents as part of a self-serving elite that has betrayed the people. This creates the justification for a leader to present themselves as the only true voice of the nation. Then, populists identify an internal enemy, often a marginalized group or political faction, or even the "deep state," and use it as a scapegoat for the country's problems. This is done in a five-step process:[3]

1. Demonize the opposition (portrayed not as a competing political force but as a threat to national stability).
2. Attack and control the media (fake news), until trust in independent journalism collapses.
3. Purge the judiciary (replace independent judges with party loyalists).
4. Gain control of state institutions (seek partisan control of the civil service, police, and military).
5. Intimidate civil society (silence voluntary organizations, trade unions, artists, and intellectuals).

These steps do not happen all at once. They unfold gradually, often disguised as necessary reforms. By the time the public realizes the extent of the power shift, democracy has already been hollowed out from within. This creates a cycle that erodes trust in institutions and makes democratic governance nearly impossible.

WHAT HAPPENS IF WE CAN'T REVERSE COURSE

Rising economic nationalism across the West threatens both stability and democracy. Policies based on isolationism—high tariffs, protectionism, and tax cuts for the wealthy—disrupt markets, raise consumer costs, and concentrate power among elites. History shows these strategies fail to deliver sustained growth, instead fueling inequality and public disillusionment. As nations retreat from global trade and cooperation, they risk economic stagnation, political instability, and a deeper turn toward authoritarianism.

As democratic institutions weaken and economic policies become more erratic, individuals must take practical steps to safeguard their financial security, mobility, and autonomy. The goal is not panic-driven hoarding but strategic planning that reduces dependence on fragile systems and prepares for a future where governments may become more interventionist, economies less predictable, and opportunities more constrained.

Relying solely on assets tied to one country—whether through property, savings, or investments—exposes individuals to significant risk if policies shift unpredictably. Diversification across multiple asset classes and jurisdictions is essential. Popular economic safe havens include Switzerland, Singapore, and, more recently, Abu Dhabi in the United Arab Emirates. Real estate in politically stable regions with strong property rights can serve as both an investment and a hedge against financial instability. However, land ownership alone is insufficient—liquidity matters. Holding a mix of foreign equities, commodities, and secure offshore financial instruments can provide flexibility if capital controls or punitive taxation policies emerge.

Cryptocurrencies offer another layer of diversification, particularly for those concerned about government overreach in financial markets. While highly volatile, decentralized assets like Bitcoin provide a store of value that cannot be easily seized or devalued by inflationary monetary policies. However, this strategy requires careful management, as regulatory scrutiny is increasing. Balancing digital assets with more stable stores of wealth, such as precious metals or foreign currency holdings, reduces risk exposure.

In uncertain political climates, having options beyond a single jurisdiction is crucial. A second passport or residency in a stable country provides the ability to relocate if conditions deteriorate. Many nations offer residency-by-investment programs, and while these require upfront capital, they provide long-term security. Similarly, maintaining foreign bank accounts and international business ties can ensure continued financial access if domestic banking systems become unreliable or restrictive.

Immigration firm Henley and Partners saw a 60% increase in applications from US citizens in a year span and in an interview with *Barron's*, Dominic Volek, global head of private clients, stated, "If you have the financial capacity, you should be as diversified in terms of your domicile options as possible, because nowhere is perfect."[4]

For those without the means to secure residency through investment, building professional skills that allow for remote work or international employability is a practical alternative. Governments that turn inward often impose restrictions on labor markets, capital flows, and even personal freedoms. A portable skill set—particularly in industries that are not heavily regulated—ensures greater autonomy and resilience against shifting policies.

As governments face growing fiscal pressures, higher taxes, wealth redistribution policies, and more aggressive regulation become likely. Reducing dependency on state-backed financial support—whether through pensions, public healthcare, or subsidies—can prevent financial hardship if these systems become unsustainable. Private insurance, diversified income streams, and investments that generate passive revenue help mitigate reliance on state-controlled economic structures.

Beyond financial considerations, physical resilience matters. Supply-chain disruptions, inflation, and economic instability can impact daily life in unexpected ways. Ensuring access to basic necessities—whether through strategic relocation, community-based support systems, or investments in essential infrastructure—adds an extra layer of security.

Remaining informed is just as important as financial preparation. Governments often implement policy changes gradually, and those who act early have the most flexibility. Monitoring shifts in taxation, capital controls, and international regulations can provide an early warning system for those considering relocation or financial restructuring.

More importantly, agility matters. Static strategies—such as merely acquiring physical assets—may prove insufficient in a rapidly changing political landscape. Instead, cultivating adaptability through continuous skill development, financial flexibility, and legal mobility ensures that individuals are not caught unprepared.

Protecting one's financial and personal future in an era of political and economic uncertainty is not about doomsday scenarios—it is about pragmatism. The best strategies involve diversification, mobility, and reducing exposure to centralized control. Those who take proactive steps now will have the flexibility to navigate an unpredictable future, while those who wait may find their options disappearing when they need them most.

AN IRREVERSIBLE COURSE?

Earlier, we said that shifting course was nearly impossible. However, there are ways to fix a broken system before it is too late. If we look back at the five-step process outlined earlier, we see that democratic erosion is not yet complete—but the window to act is closing. The survival of democracy hinges on three pillars: strong institutions, an informed and engaged public, and an economy that creates and distributes wealth equitably.

Democratic resilience depends on strong institutions, legal safeguards, and civic engagement. Independent courts, separation of powers, and nonpartisan regulatory agencies prevent leaders from dismantling democracy. Reforms must reinforce these protections, ensuring institutions serve the public, not political interests.

Populists exploit weak institutions by rewriting rules to consolidate power. Democracies must close these loopholes with stronger safeguards: supermajorities for constitutional changes, limits on executive control over watchdog agencies, and automatic legal triggers to block power grabs. Without these, institutions exist in name only. Democratic stability depends on more than laws—it requires public vigilance and civic engagement. Courts, voters, and civil society must keep leaders in check. Without active public oversight, legal protections mean little. Strengthening civic education, improving meritocracy, securing elections, and enforcing financial transparency deter corruption and reinforce democratic stability.

An informed, engaged public is democracy's best defense. Populism thrives on misinformation, but public awareness can neutralize its impact. Civil society, independent media, and grassroots movements must expose propaganda and defend institutional integrity. Restoring trust in credible journalism and countering digital disinformation are essential to slowing democratic erosion. Resistance, not complacency, determines whether democracy survives.

Voting is not just a right; it is the foundation of political accountability. Low voter turnout weakens democracy, allowing a small, highly motivated ideological minority to wield disproportionate influence. This leads to political polarization and government policies that do not reflect the will of the broader population. In the US, voter turnout has been alarmingly low in local and midterm elections, sometimes dipping below 40%. This enables political extremism to thrive, as elections are often decided by the most ideologically committed voters rather than a broad representation of the public.

Beyond voting, civic engagement plays a critical role in sustaining democracy. A healthy democracy requires more than periodic elections—an informed and engaged public holds leaders accountable. Over time, civic participation has declined, with fewer citizens attending public meetings, joining community organizations, or volunteering for political causes. This erosion of "social capital" makes democracy more vulnerable, as disengaged citizens are less likely to challenge misinformation, resist authoritarian tendencies, or demand transparency from their leaders. Encouraging greater civic involvement, whether through national service programs, local activism, or participatory policy discussions, is essential for reversing this trend. When citizens feel empowered to shape their political system beyond just casting a ballot, democracy becomes more resilient against populist manipulation and institutional decay.

Wealth creation and distribution also shape democracy's survival. Extreme inequality fuels discontent, concentrating both money and political power in the hands of a few. A thriving middle class stabilizes society, broadens economic opportunity, and reduces populist appeal. Policies that promote education, social mobility, and fair taxation prevent wealth from becoming a tool of political dominance. While AI has been a point of contention in this book, it does have its advantages. When combined with other emerging technologies like virtual reality and 5G capabilities, AI has the potential to reduce the costs of education, healthcare, and government programs. Without shared prosperity, democracy weakens.

Policymakers must expand opportunity through progressive taxation, education investment, and policies that support upward mobility. Affordable housing and healthcare prevent economic despair, while campaign finance reforms curb money's outsized influence in politics. Broadly shared growth fosters trust in government and weakens populist extremism. This all sounds good in theory but enacting real change will be difficult. Political inertia, entrenched interests, and public distrust make reform an uphill battle. If we fail to act, inequality will deepen, institutions will weaken, and democracy will erode.

This is not a call to despair but a recognition of reality. The future may be uncertain, but it is not yet decided. Democratic systems, though battered, still offer a path forward—one that depends on engaged citizens refusing to be divided by fear and distraction. Populists thrive on chaos, but history shows that when people recognize failure and corruption, they push back. The strength of democracy lies not in its permanence, but in its ability to be reclaimed. Even when weakened, democracy retains the power to correct course.

"A republic, if you can keep it."
   –Benjamin Franklin, when asked *"What kind of government have you delivered us?"*

NOTES

CHAPTER 1

1. Freedom House. *Freedom in the World 2025: Scores and Status*. Accessed January 21, 2025. https://freedomhouse.org/countries/freedomworld/scores?sort=desc&order=Total%20Score%20and%20Status.
2. Freedom House. *Freedom in the World 2025: Scores and Status*. Accessed January 21, 2025. https://freedomhouse.org/countries/freedomworld/scores?sort=desc&order=Total%20Score%20and%20Status.
3. World Bank. "Investing in Youth: Transforming Africa's Future." *World Bank*, June 27, 2023. https://www.worldbank.org/en/news/feature/2023/06/27/investing-in-youth-transforming-afe-africa.
4. Congressional Research Service. *China's Economic Rise: History, Trends, Challenges, and Implications for the United States*. Washington, DC: Congressional Research Service, 2021. https://www.everycrsreport.com/reports/RL33534.html.
5. NATO. *Defence Expenditure of NATO Countries (2014–2024)*. NATO Public Diplomacy Division, June 17, 2024.

6. Düben, B.A. "Revising History and 'Gathering the Russian Lands': Vladimir Putin and Ukrainian Nationhood." *LSE Public Policy Review*, 3(1), (2023), 4. Available at: https://doi.org/10.31389/lseppr.86.
7. NATO. *Defence Expenditure of NATO Countries (2014–2024)*. NATO Public Diplomacy Division, June 17, 2024.
8. V-Dem, *V-Dem Country-Year (Full + Others) v14* [dataset], processed by Our World in Data, 2024. Accessed January 21, 2025. https://ourworldindata.org/democracy.
9. International Monetary Fund. *Regional Economic Outlook: Asia and Pacific: Challenges to Sustaining Growth and Disinflation*. World Economic and Financial Surveys. Washington, DC: International Monetary Fund, 2023.
10. Madden, Jerry. *Steel Valley: Coming of Age in the Ohio Valley in the 1960s*. Potomac Publishing Company, 2023.
11. Madden, Jerry. *Steel Valley: Coming of Age in the Ohio Valley in the 1960s*. Potomac Publishing Company, 2023.
12. McMahon, Dinny. *China's Great Wall of Debt: Shadow Banks, Ghost Cities, Massive Loans, and the End of the Chinese Miracle*. Boston: Houghton Mifflin Harcourt, 2018.
13. McMahon, Dinny. *China's Great Wall of Debt: Shadow Banks, Ghost Cities, Massive Loans, and the End of the Chinese Miracle*. Boston: Houghton Mifflin Harcourt, 2018.
14. Bertelsmann Stiftung. *Globalization Report 2020: The Most Important Facts in 5 Charts*. Global Europe, 2020. https://globaleurope.eu/globalization/globalization-report-2020-the-most-important-facts-in-5-charts/.
15. People's Republic of China, State Council. *Made in China 2025*. May 8, 2015. Translated by Etcetera Language Group, Inc. Edited by Ben Murphy, CSET Translation Manager. Accessed February 2025. https://perma.cc/9PA3-WYBA.

16. Miller, Chris. *Chip War: The Fight for the World's Most Critical Technology*. New York: Scribner, 2022.

CHAPTER 2

1. CEIC. *United States Government Debt (% of Nominal GDP)*. CEIC Data, September 2024. https://www.ceicdata.com/en/indicator/united-states/government-debt--of-nominal-gdp.
2. McMahon, Dinny. *China's Great Wall of Debt: Shadow Banks, Ghost Cities, Massive Loans, and the End of the Chinese Miracle*. Boston: Houghton Mifflin Harcourt, 2018.
3. McMahon, Dinny. *China's Great Wall of Debt: Shadow Banks, Ghost Cities, Massive Loans, and the End of the Chinese Miracle*. Boston: Houghton Mifflin Harcourt, 2018.
4. McMahon, Dinny. *China's Great Wall of Debt: Shadow Banks, Ghost Cities, Massive Loans, and the End of the Chinese Miracle*. Boston: Houghton Mifflin Harcourt, 2018.
5. World Bank and OECD. *World Bank National Accounts Data and OECD National Accounts Data Files*. Accessed January 25, 2025. https://data.worldbank.org/country/china.

CHAPTER 3

1. European Parliament. *Political Groups in the European Parliament: Historical Evolution (1979–1994)*. European Parliament Historical Archives. Accessed February 12, 2025. https://historicalarchives.europarl.europa.eu/files/live/sites/historicalarchive/files/03_PUBLICATIONS/03_European-Parliament/01_Documents/political-groups-in-the-european-parliament-en.pdf.

NOTES

2. Organisation for Economic Co-operation and Development (OECD). *International Migration Outlook 2024: Germany.* OECD Publishing, 2024. https://www.oecd.org/en/publications/2024/11/international-migration-outlook-2024_c6f3e803/full-report/germany_1c19b40c.html.
3. International Organization for Migration (IOM). *World Migration Report 2024: Europe.* IOM, 2024. https://worldmigrationreport.iom.int/what-we-do/world-migration-report-2024-chapter-3/europe.
4. Pew Research Center. *Key Facts About Recent Trends in Global Migration.* December 16, 2022. https://www.pewresearch.org/short-reads/2022/12/16/key-facts-about-recent-trends-in-global-migration/.
5. Geis-Thöne, Wido. Die Bedeutung der Zuwanderung für den wirtschaftlichen Erfolg Deutschlands. IW-Analyse, Nr. 151, Köln, 2022.
6. Bánkuti, Miklós, Gábor Halmai, and Kim Lane Scheppele. "Hungary's Illiberal Turn: Disabling the Constitution." *Journal of Democracy*, 23(3), (2012), 138–146. https://dx.doi.org/10.1353/jod.2012.0054.

CHAPTER 4

1. Couzin, Iain. "On Fish, Fascists, and the Power of Collective Behaviour." Lecture, Science & Cocktails, Paradiso Noord, Amsterdam, March 8, 2023.
2. Couzin, Iain. "On Fish, Fascists, and the Power of Collective Behaviour." Lecture, Science & Cocktails, Paradiso Noord, Amsterdam, March 8, 2023.
3. Thomas, Merlyn, and Mike Wendling. "Trump Repeats Baseless Claim About Haitian Immigrants Eating Pets." *BBC News*, September 15, 2024. https://www.bbc.com/news/articles/c77l28myezko.

Notes

4. Amnesty International USA. "Facebook's Systems Promoted Violence Against Rohingya," 2022. https://www.amnestyusa.org/reports/facebook-systems-promoted-violence-against-rohingya/.

5. Fisher, Max. *The Chaos Machine: The Inside Story of How Social Media Rewired Our Minds and Our World.* New York: Little, Brown and Company, 2022.

6. Harris, Johnny. How Facebook Became a Tool for Genocide. YouTube video, 24:10. Posted October 18, 2023. https://www.youtube.com/watch?v=K8B0bWO9u3M.

7. Carnegie Endowment for International Peace. "Facebook, Telegram, and the Ongoing Struggle Against Online Hate Speech," September 2023. https://carnegieendowment.org/research/2023/09/facebook-telegram-and-the-ongoing-struggle-against-online-hate-speech?lang=en.

8. Amnesty International USA. "Facebook's Systems Promoted Violence Against Rohingya," 2022. https://www.amnestyusa.org/reports/facebook-systems-promoted-violence-against-rohingya/.

9. Hannah Beech. "UN Blames Facebook for Spreading Hatred of Rohingya in Myanmar." *Time*, March 12, 2018. https://time.com/5197039/un-facebook-myanmar-rohingya-violence/.

10. Amnesty International. "Myanmar: Facebook's Systems Promoted Violence Against Rohingya–Meta Owes Reparations," September 2022. https://www.amnesty.org/en/latest/news/2022/09/myanmar-facebooks-systems-promoted-violence-against-rohingya-meta-owes-reparations-new-report/.

11. Associated Press. "Slovakia's Fico to Form Government, Set to Stop Military Aid to Ukraine." *Associated Press*, October 25, 2023. https://apnews.com/article/slovakia-fico-new-government-0e36d0bac400f6bfca529bd10f5b81cd.

NOTES

12. Jochecová, Ketrin, and Nicolas Camut. "Slovakia, the EU's Next Rule of Law Headache." *Politico EU*, March 20, 2024. https://www.politico.eu/article/slovakia-eu-rule-of-law-prime-minister-robert-fico/.
13. Radio Free Europe/Radio Liberty. "Romanian Elections Targeted by 'Aggressive Hybrid Russian Action,' Declassified Documents Show," December 4, 2024. https://www.rferl.org/a/romania-russia-election-interference-tiktok/33227010.html.
14. International Monetary Fund. *World Economic Outlook: October 2024*. IMF, 2024. https://www.imf.org/external/datamapper/NGDPD@WEO.

CHAPTER 5

1. Field, Hayden. "DeepSeek's Hardware Spend Could Be as High as $500 Million, New Report Estimates." *CNBC*, January 31, 2025. https://www.cnbc.com/amp/2025/01/31/deepseeks-hardware-spend-could-be-as-high-as-500-million-report.html.
2. Shin, Jieun. "AI and Misinformation." *2024 Dean's Report*, University of Florida.
3. Warzel, Charlie. "People Aren't Falling for AI Trump Photos (Yet)." *The Atlantic*, March 24, 2023.
4. Christopher, Nilesh. "The Near Future of Deepfakes Just Got Way Clearer." *The Atlantic*, June 5, 2024.
5. Simon, Felix M., Sacha Altay, and Hugo Mercier. "Misinformation Reloaded? Fears about the Impact of Generative AI on Misinformation Are Overblown." *Harvard Kennedy School Misinformation Review*, October 2023.
6. IBISWorld. *Telemarketing & Call Centers in the US - Market Research Report*, January 2025. Accessed February 1, 2025. https://www.ibisworld.com/united-states/industry/telemarketing-call-centers/1468/.

7. Reuters. "Sweden's Klarna Says AI Chatbots Help Shrink Headcount." *Reuters*, August 27, 2024. https://www.reuters.com/technology/artificial-intelligence/swedens-klarna-says-ai-chatbots-help-shrink-headcount-2024-08-27/.
8. Mollick, Ethan. *Co-Intelligence: Living and Working with AI*. New York: Penguin Random House, 2024.
9. Field, Hayden. "DeepSeek's Hardware Spend Could Be as High as $500 Million, New Report Estimates." *CNBC*, January 31, 2025. https://www.cnbc.com/amp/2025/01/31/deepseeks-hardware-spend-could-be-as-high-as-500-million-report.html.
10. Roche, David. "DeepSeek—Deeply Seeking the Significance." *Quantum Strategy Report*, 2024.
11. The Economist. "How Ukraine Uses Cheap AI-Guided Drones to Deadly Effect Against Russia." *The Economist*, 2024.

CHAPTER 6

1. Roche, David. "Four Quartets." *Quantum Strategy*, April 20–23, 2021.
2. Mahbubani, Kishore. "Measuring the Power of the Global South." *The World Today*, Chatham House, February 2024. https://www.chathamhouse.org/publications/the-world-today/2024-02/measuring-power-global-south.
3. Sweijs, Tim, and Michael J. Mazarr. "Mind the Middle Powers." *War on the Rocks*, April 4, 2023. https://warontherocks.com/2023/04/mind-the-middle-powers/.
4. Foa, Roberto, Margot Mollat, Xavier Romero-Vidal, Han Isha, David Evans, and Andrew Klassen. *A World Divided: Russia, China and the West*. Cambridge: Bennett Institute for Public Policy, University of Cambridge, October 20, 2022. https://www.bennettinstitute.cam.ac.uk/publications/a-world-divided/.

NOTES

5. Cash, Joe. "China, Saudi Arabia Sign Currency Swap Agreement." *Reuters*, November 20, 2023. https://www.reuters.com/markets/currencies/china-saudi-arabia-central-banks-sign-local-currency-swap-agreement-2023-11-20/.

6. Hoang, Thi Ha, and Pham Thi Phuong Thao. "Re-ordering the World: China's Global South Focus versus the Ally-Centric Approach of the US." *ISEAS Perspective*, No. 2024/90, September 2024. ISEAS–Yusof Ishak Institute. https://www.iseas.edu.sg/articles-commentaries/iseas-perspective/2024-90-re-ordering-the-world-chinas-global-south-focus-versus-the-ally-centric-approach-of-the-us-by-hoang-thi-ha-and-pham-thi-phuong-thao/.

7. Masters, Jonathan, and Will Merrow. "How Much U.S. Aid Is Going to Ukraine?" *Council on Foreign Relations*, September 27, 2024. https://www.cfr.org/article/how-much-us-aid-going-ukraine.

8. Eichengreen, Barry, Arnaud J. Mehl, and Livia Chitu. "Mars or Mercury? The Geopolitics of International Currency Choice." NBER Working Paper 24145, December 2017.

9. Japan Times, "Japan to Boost Defense Budget to ¥43 Trillion over Five Years, Exceeding 2% of GDP." *The Japan Times*, December 3, 2022; Perun. "Japanese Defence Strategy & Rearmament - Japan's Ambitious Plans & Lessons from Ukraine." YouTube video, 38:42. January 18, 2023. https://youtu.be/2BHnijL9xYc. Ministry of Defense, Japan. Defence of Japan 2022 (White Paper). Accessed January 21, 2025. https://www.mod.go.jp/en/publ/w_paper/index.html; ARTE. "Japan Preparing for War." YouTube video, 26:13. August 15, 2023. https://youtu.be/q-g9RyJm9y8.

10. McKinsey & Company. "Taking the Pulse of Shifting Supply Chains," August 2022. https://www.mckinsey.com/industries/operations/our-insights/taking-the-pulse-of-shifting-supply-chains.

Notes

11. Attinasi, Maria-Grazia, Lukas Boeckelmann, and Baptiste Meunier. "Friend-Shoring Global Value Chains: A Model-Based Assessment." *ECB Economic Bulletin*, 2, (2023).
12. Dario Caldara, Sarah Conlisk, Matteo Iacoviello, and Maddie Penn, "Do Geopolitical Risks Raise or Lower Inflation?" *Board of Governors of the Federal Reserve System*, February 15, 2023. https://www.federalreserve.gov/econres/2023-geopolitical-risks-and-inflation.htm.
13. Caldara, Dario, Sarah Conlisk, Matteo Iacoviello, and Maddie Penn. "Do Geopolitical Risks Raise or Lower Inflation?" *Board of Governors of the Federal Reserve System*, February 15, 2023. https://www.federalreserve.gov/econres/2023-geopolitical-risks-and-inflation.htm.
14. International Monetary Fund. *Currency Composition of Official Foreign Exchange Reserves (COFER)*. Accessed February 2025. https://data.imf.org/?sId=1442948906947&sk=E6A5F467-C14B-4AA8-9F6D-5A09EC4E62A4.
15. Naef, Alain, Eric Monnet, Camille Macaire, Arnaud Mehl, and Barry Eichengreen. "The Renminbi's Unconventional Route to Reserve Currency Status." *VOXEU*, October 31, 2022. https://voxeu.org/article/renminbi-s-unconventional-route-reserve-currency-status.
16. SWIFT. RMB Tracker: Renminbi's Progress as an International Currency – June 2024. La Hulpe, Belgium: Society for Worldwide Interbank Financial Telecommunication, July 2024. https://www.swift.com/news-events/rmb-tracker.
17. Weiss, Colin. *Geopolitics and the U.S. Dollar's Future as a Reserve Currency*. International Finance Discussion Papers No. 1359. Washington, DC: Board of Governors of the Federal Reserve System, October 2022. https://www.federalreserve.gov/econres/ifdp/files/ifdp1359.pdf.
18. Weiss, Colin. *Geopolitics and the U.S. Dollar's Future as a Reserve Currency*. International Finance Discussion Papers No. 1359.

Washington, DC: Board of Governors of the Federal Reserve System, October 2022. https://www.federalreserve.gov/econres/ifdp/files/ifdp1359.pdf.

19. Applebaum, Anne. *Autocracy, Inc.: The Dictators Who Want to Run the World*. New York: Doubleday, 2024.

CHAPTER 7

1. Saad, Lydia. "Inflation, Immigration Rank Among Top U.S. Issue Concerns." *Gallup News*, March 29, 2024. https://news.gallup.com/poll/642887/inflation-immigration-rank-among-top-issue-concerns.aspx.
2. Thatcher, Margaret. "Speeches to the Conservative Party Conference, 1975–78." In *CPC, 1989*, 19–28. Thatcher Archive. https://www.margaretthatcher.org/document/103105.
3. Statista. *United States: Share of Global Gross Domestic Product (GDP) from 2010 to 2029*. Accessed February 2025. https://www.statista.com/statistics/270267/united-states-share-of-global-gross-domestic-product-gdp/.
4. Cloud, Marcus. "The Default of Russia in 1998: What Happened Actually?" *iLaw Journals*, March 9, 2020. https://www.ilawjournals.com/the-default-of-russia-in-1998-what-happened-actually/?utm.
5. Mete Feridun. "Russian Financial Crisis of 1998: An Econometric Investigation." *International Journal of Applied Econometrics and Quantitative Studies*, 1(4), (2004), 113.
6. Pinto, Brian, and Ulatov, Sergei. *Financial Globalization and the Russian Crisis of 1998*. Policy Research Working Paper 5312. Washington, DC: The World Bank, Europe and Central Asia Region and The Managing Director's Office, May 2010.

7. "Historical Tables." *Office of Management and Budget.* Obama White House Archives. https://obamawhitehouse.archives.gov/omb/budget/Historicals.

CHAPTER 8

1. Peri, Giovanni. "Can Immigration Solve the Demographic Dilemma?" *IMF Finance & Development,* March 2020. https://www.imf.org/en/Publications/fandd/issues/2020/03/can-immigration-solve-the-demographic-dilemma-peri.
2. Partnership for a New American Economy. *"Patent Pending: How Immigrants Are Reinventing the American Economy,"* June 26, 2012. https://www.newamericaneconomy.org/wp-content/uploads/2013/07/patent-pending.pdf.
3. International Monetary Fund. "Migration to Advanced Economies Can Raise Growth." *IMF Blog.* June 19, 2020. https://www.imf.org/en/Blogs/Articles/2020/06/19/blog-weo-chapter4-migration-to-advanced-economies-can-raise-growth.
4. Peri, Giovanni. "Can Immigration Solve the Demographic Dilemma?" *IMF Finance & Development,* March 2020. https://www.imf.org/en/Publications/fandd/issues/2020/03/can-immigration-solve-the-demographic-dilemma-peri.
5. United Nations Department of Economic and Social Affairs, Population Division (2022). *World Population Prospects 2022: Summary of Results.* UN DESA/POP/2022/TR/NO. 3.
6. World Health Organization. *GHE: Life Expectancy and Healthy Life Expectancy.* Accessed February 2025. https://www.who.int/data/gho/data/themes/mortality-and-global-health-estimates/ghe-life-expectancy-and-healthy-life-expectancy.

7. Central Intelligence Agency. "Life Expectancy at Birth–Country Comparison." *The World Factbook*. Accessed February 2025. https://www.cia.gov/the-world-factbook/field/life-expectancy-at-birth/country-comparison/.
8. McDermott, John. "The Economic Gap Between Africa and the Rest of the World Is Growing." *The Economist*, January 6, 2025. https://www.economist.com/special-report/2025/01/06/the-economic-gap-between-africa-and-the-rest-of-the-world-is-growing.
9. "The Globalization of Indifference: Pope Francis Asks, 'Who Is Responsible?'" *JustSouth Monthly*, October 2013. Jesuit Social Research Institute, Loyola University New Orleans. Accessed January 25, 2025. https://jsri.loyno.edu/sites/loyno.edu.jsri/files/October%202013.pdf.
10. Nowrasteh, Alex, and Michelangelo Landgrave. "Criminal Immigrants in 2020: Their Numbers, Demographics, and Economic Impact." Migration Policy Institute, 2020. https://www.migrationpolicy.org/content/immigrants-and-crime.
11. Light, Michael T., and Ty Miller. "Does Undocumented Immigration Increase Violent Crime?" *Proceedings of the National Academy of Sciences*, 117(15) (April 14, 2020), 8828–8834. https://www.pnas.org/doi/10.1073/pnas.2014704117.
12. Caselli, Francesca, Huidan Lin, Frederik Toscani, and Jiaxiong Yao. "Migration into the EU: Stocktaking of Recent Developments and Macroeconomic Implications." *IMF Working Paper* No. 24/211. International Monetary Fund, September 27, 2024. https://www.imf.org/en/Publications/WP/Issues/2024/09/27/Migration-into-the-EU-Stocktaking-of-Recent-Developments-and-Macroeconomic-Implications-555578.
13. Migration Observatory. *The Fiscal Impact of Immigration in the UK*. University of Oxford. Accessed January 24, 2025. https://migrationobservatory.ox.ac.uk/resources/briefings/the-fiscal-impact-of-immigration-in-the-uk/.

Notes

CHAPTER 9

1. Norwich University. *The Cost of US Wars–Then & Now*. Accessed January 24, 2025. https://online.norwich.edu/resource/war/cost-us-wars.
2. "NATO's Combined GDP Is Far Larger than Russia's." *World Economics*. Last modified January 5, 2025. https://www.worldeconomics.com/Thoughts/NATOs-Combined-GDP-is-far-larger-than-Russias.aspx.
3. *Freedom in the World 2024: Digital Booklet*. Freedom House, February 2024. Accessed January 25, 2025. https://freedomhouse.org/sites/default/files/2024-02/FIW_2024_DigitalBooklet.pdf.
4. Heller, Peter S. "Wealth Creation and Social Justice: An IMF Perspective." Speaking notes prepared for the World Council of Churches – World Bank – IMF Meeting, Geneva, February 13–14, 2003. International Monetary Fund, 2003.
5. Duina, Francesco. *States and Nations, Power and Civility: Hallsian Perspectives*. Toronto: University of Toronto Press, 2018.
6. "Happiest Countries in the World 2024." *World Population Review*, January 25, 2025. https://worldpopulationreview.com/country-rankings/happiest-countries-in-the-world.
7. World Bank. *Gini Index (World Bank Estimate)*. Accessed February 2025. https://data.worldbank.org/indicator/SI.POV.GINI.

CHAPTER 10

1. Levitsky, Steven, and Daniel Ziblatt. *How Democracies Die*. New York: Crown, 2018.
2. Levitsky, Steven, and Daniel Ziblatt. *How Democracies Die*. New York: Crown, 2018.

NOTES

3. Diamond, Larry. *The Spirit of Democracy: The Struggle to Build Free Societies Throughout the World*. New York: Times Books/Henry Holt and Co., 2008.
4. Schultz, Abby. "The Rich Are Moving Assets Abroad. What's Prompting the Shift." *Barron's*, February 5, 2025. https://www.barrons.com/articles/rich-investments-assets-abroad-trump-politics-04d01203.

INDEX

Page numbers followed by *f* refer to figures.

A
Abu Dabi, 157
Africa, 4, 137–138
Allen, Danielle, 155
Alliances, 34
    Alliance of Democracies, 4–6
    Axis of Autocracies, 4–14
    global, formation of, 103–107, 103*f*, 106*f*
    and global currency dynamics, 114–115
Alliance of Democracies, 4–6, 145. *See also* Grayzone
Arendt, Hannah, 73
Artificial intelligence (AI), 81–99, 161
    discourse affected by, 84–88
    as double-edged sword, 98–99
    as global arms race, 92–94
    job market affected by, 89–92
    and perception of reality, 152–153
    in warfare, 94–97
Asian nations, 115, 137
Assad, Bashar al-, 11
Australia, 115
Authoritarianism, 15, 17, 18*f*
    and AI race, 98
    digital, 94
    and isolationism, 156
    normalization of, 56
Autocracies, 18*f*
    democracies vs., 1, 3–6, 5*f* (*See also* Grayzone)
    populists aligned with, 59
    pros and cons of, 38–39
Axis of Autocracies, 4–14. *See also* Grayzone
    countries in, 4, 6–11
    democracies undermined by, 79–80
    disinformation campaigns of, 74–80
    and Fascist Axis of 1930s, 144–145
    path to victory against, 145
    threat posed by, 11–14
    and Ukraine war, 11–12
    and USD in global finance, 121

INDEX

B
Big government, 35
BRICS, 103, 104

C
Callamard, Agnès, 73
China:
  in AI race, 82, 92–95
  autocratic model of, 2, 2f, 4
  in *Axis of Autocracies*, 4, 7–9, 12
  and currency warfare, 104–105, 112–116
  disinformation from, 75
  election interference by, 78
  end of economic miracle in, 24–25, 36–41
  and globalization, 18–20, 24–27, 51, 107–108
  in Grayzone, 101–107, 109
Ciolacu, Marcel, 78
Civic engagement, 159–161
Cold War, 15–16, 45, 101
Collective behavior, 62–65
Crimea, 76
Currency warfare, 110–117

D
Deglobalization, 25, 33–34, 108
Democracy(-ies), 18f. *See also Alliance of Democracies*
  in AI race, 92, 96, 98
  autocracies vs., 1, 3–6, 5f (*See also* Grayzone)
  core values of, 154
  external challenges to, 1–27
  freedom in, 1–3, 3f
  future of, 151–161
  in Grayzone, 101
  immigration policies in, 141
  internal decay of, 29–41
  populism vs., 51–54, 52f, 53f
  unwritten norms of, 153–154
  US as global promoter of, 5
  without ethnic majority, 155
Democratization:
  of AI-driven warfare, 97
  and globalization, 17, 18f, 21
D'Estaing, Giscard, 130
Diamond, Larry, 155
Discourse:
  AI's effect on, 84–88
  as threat to democracy, 31–33
Disinformation, 74–80
Douglas, Stephen, 32
Duina, Francesco, 147

E
Economic prosperity, 2, 3
Economy(-ies):
  of China, 4, 5f, 7–8, 24–27, 36–41
  and globalization, 16–27, 108
  and immigration, 135–137
  of Iran, 10
  militarizing, 110
  of Russia, 79, 128
  of United States, 126–127
Egypt, 112
Election interference, 75–78, 86

180

Emerging economies:
   and globalization, 17–27
   and Grayzone, 104, 119
Equality, 154, 155, 161
Europe:
   aid to Ukraine, 143
   in AI race, 93
   in *Alliance of Democracies*, 115
   apprenticeships in, 50
   immigrants in, 140–141
   political parties in, 45–49
   populist politicians in, 58–59
   security/stability in, 101, 102
European Union (EU), 115, 130, 131
Expansionism:
   by China, 8–9
   by Russia, 6–7, 14, 76–79
External challenges, 1–27
   Axis of Autocracies, 4–14
   and Cold War, 15–16
   globalization, 17–27, 18f, 19f
   Grayzone, 3–6, 5f, 27, 101–119

F
Fico, Robert, 75–76
Financial safeguards, 157–158
Finland, 148, 149
Fiscal challenges, 158
   currency warfare, 110–117
   government spending, 35
   with immigration, 136–138
France, 46, 138, 139
Francis, Pope, 139

Franklin, Benjamin, 152, 163
Freedom, 1–3, 2f, 3f
   consistent declines in, 14
   as core democratic value, 154
   and wealth distribution, 147
Friedman, Thomas, 66
Future of democracy, 151–161
   fixing the broken system, 159–161
   if we can't reverse course, 156–159
   issues concerning, 152–156

G
Geopolitical dominance, 6–7, 92–94, 101
Georgescu, Calin, 78
Georgia, 76, 77, 145
Germany:
   aging population in, 134
   GDP per capita in, 25
   immigration measures in, 138–139
   populism in, 30, 46–51, 59
   and Russian aggression, 77
Globalization:
   collapse of, 107–110
   level playing field with, 66
   and populism, 50–51
   as threat to democracies, 17–27, 18f, 19f
   worker benefits with, 140
Global reserve currency, 111–113
   creation of, 129–132
   and currency warfare, 110–117
   USD as, 116, 121–122

INDEX

Global South, 3–4, 103, 104, 119
Governments:
  active interventions by, 107–110
  conflicts created by, 39
  role of, 149
Government spending, 35, 40–41
Grayzone, 3–6, 5f, 27, 101–119
  balance of power in, 98
  in currency warfare, 110–117
  disinformation campaigns, 74–80
  and formation of global alliances, 103–107, 103f, 106f
  and outcomes of multi-polar world, 107–110
  trickle-down effects of, 117–119
  warfare in, 3–6, 5f, 80, 102, 117–118
Greece, 131

H
Higgins, Eliot, 85
Hungary, 56, 57

I
Immigrants:
  and aging population, 134–137
  false claims about, 69–70
  in Germany, 47–49
Immigration, 47, 133–142
  benefits of, 140–142
  economic challenges with, 135–137
  fiscal challenges with, 136–138
  global reactions to, 138–140
  as populist issue, 133–134

India, 18, 86, 104, 114
Industries:
  Chinese, 37, 38
  and globalization, 16–27, 50–51, 108
  impact of AI on, 89–92
Information flow, 65–68, 153
Institutions, strength of, 159–160
Internal democratic decay, 14, 29–41, 152–156
  big government, 35
  deglobalization, 33–34
  discourse, 31–33
  end of China's economic miracle, 36–41
  populism, 29–31
  social media and, 80
Iran, 4, 10–11, 75
Italy, 31, 46, 58
Ivanishvili, Bidzina, 76

J
January 6th Capitol attack, 70–71, 152
Japan:
  aging population in, 134
  in *Alliance of Democracies*, 4, 115
  conflicts created by, 40
  defense ambitions of, 108–109
  life expectancy in, 136
Job market(s), 89–92, 135, 137

K
Kasparov, Garry, 73
Kažimír, Peter, 76

182

Kim Jong Un, 9
Kováčik, Dušan, 76
Kurzweil, Ray, 82

L
Labor arbitrage, 16, 107–108
Labor markets, 17–27, 48, 50
Lagarde, Christine, 110
Legal safeguards, 159, 160
Levitsky, Steven, 152–155
Lincoln, Abraham, 32

M
McMahon, Dinny, 24, 37
Maduro, Nicolás, 57
Malthus, Thomas, 135–136
Meloni, Giorgio, 31, 58
Merkel, Angela, 47, 50, 51, 77
Military dominance, 27, 94–97
Military spending, 40–41, 108, 110, 143
Misinformation:
    AI-driven, 84–88, 153
    neutralizing, 160
    on social media, 68–74
Moldova, 77, 145
Musk, Elon, 49, 68
Myanmar, 72–73

N
NATO countries, 4–5, 14, 45, 115
New Zealand, 115
N-Factor states, 103–107, 106*f*, 114
North Korea, 4, 9–10

Norway, 149
Nuclear power, 9, 40, 118

O
Ódor, Ľudovít, 76
Orbán, Viktor, 57, 58

P
Papperger, Armin, 16
Personal safeguards, 158–159
Political instability, AI and, 89
Political parties, populism and, 44–49, 51–54, 52*f*, 53*f*
Political warfare, 86
Populism, 43–59
    and AI-driven job loss, 91–92
    democracy vs., 51–54, 52*f*, 53*f*
    in Germany, 46–51
    history of, 44–46
    immigration issue in, 133–134, 140, 141
    key factors in, 56
    in practice, 54–58
    in the real world, 58–59
    and social media, 44, 61, 72–74, 79
    strategy of, 155–156
    as threat to democracy, 29–31
Power:
    alignment of, 12–13
    balance of, 15–16, 98
    concentration of, 156
    and control of information, 68
    in populist regimes, 56–57

Propaganda, 73–74, 88, 153
Proxy warfare, 11, 15
Public safety, immigration and, 48
Putin, Vladimir, 6, 13, 56–57, 75, 79, 145

R
Reality, perception of, 98–99, 153
Residency options, 157–158
Resilience, 158, 159
Resource wealth, 10–11, 40
Romania, 77, 145
Russia:
   in *Axis of Autocracies*, 4, 6–7, 11–12
   in Cold War, 15–16
   debt burden of, 127–128
   disinformation from, 75–79
   election interference by, 75–78
   frozen reserves of, 114
   future for, 145–146
   in Grayzone, 101–104, 109
   recent plots by, 16
   and Ukraine war, 6–7, 77–79, 143–145 (*See also* Ukraine war)

S
Sandu, Maia, 77
Saudi Arabia, 104–105
Singapore, 157
Slovakia, 75–76, 149
Social inequality, 89
Social media, 61–80
   and collective behavior, 62–65
   confirmation bias with, 32–33, 153
   convergence of AI and, 84–88
   divisiveness of, 154
   and information landscape, 65–68
   misinformation/negative information on, 68–74
   and perception of reality, 152–153
   and populism, 44, 61, 72–74, 79
   as a weapon, 74–80
Somalia, 136
South Africa, 148
South Korea, 4, 115
Sovereign debt, 122–125, 131
Soviet Union, 15–16, 45
Stoianoglo, Alexandr, 77
Sweden, 148, 149
Switzerland, 157
Syria, 11

T
Taiwan, 2, 2f, 4, 26
Thatcher, Margaret, 124
Trade:
   global, 114
   and globalization, 16–27, 19f, 51, 110
   in multi-polar world, 108
   and USD, 125–127 (*See also* Currency warfare)
Trump, Donald, 69, 74, 85, 153

U
Ukraine war, 6–7, 143–145
   as AI testing ground, 95–96
   alliance support for, 107

Axis of Autocracies solidified by, 11–12
China's assistance in, 102
frozen Russian reserves in, 114
North Korean troops in, 9
Russian disinformation in, 77–79
US and European aid for, 143
as war of attrition, 117
United Kingdom (UK), 33, 141
United States (US):
   aging population in, 134
   in AI race, 92–95
   in *Alliance of Democracies*, 4–5
   in Cold War, 15–16
   costs of WWII for, 143
   and currency warfare, 104–105, 111–117
   debt of, 122–127, 129–130
   disaster management in, 34
   election interference in, 75
   financial dominance of, 121–122
   future of democracy in, 152–156
   in Grayzone warfare, 118
   hegemony in, 102
   immigrants in, 133, 140
   populist politicians in, 58
   support to Ukraine from, 107, 143
US dollar (USD), 121–132
   and global reserve currency, 111–113, 116, 121–122, 129–132
   and Grayzone warfare, 119
   loss of confidence in, 127–128
   and trade imbalance, 125–127
   and US's sovereign debt, 122–125

V
Venezuela, 57
Volek, Dominic, 158

W
Warfare. *See also* Ukraine war
   AI-driven, 94–97
   currency, 110–117
   disinformation in, 77–80
   and economic health, 39–40
   in Grayzone, 3–6, 5*f*, 80, 102, 117–118 (*See also* Grayzone)
   political, 86
   proxy, 11, 15
   risks of global war, 13
Wealth, 143–149
   creation and distribution of, 146–149, 161
   during Great Moderation, 109
   and Russia-Ukraine war, 143–146
Weapon(s):
   AI, 92–97
   social media as, 74–80

X
Xi Jinping, 39, 80

Z
Ziblatt, Daniel, 152–155
Zourabichvili, Salome, 76
Zuckerberg, Mark, 68